DO'S AND DON'T'S
IN
HOME STAGING
AND REDESIGN

BARBARA JENNINGS, CSS/CRS

The Academy of Staging & Redesign
Decorate-Redecorate.Com

Copyright and Disclaimer

Published by Ahava Enterprises, Inc. | Ahava Press
All rights reserved under International and Pan-American Copyright Conventions.

Library of Congress No: 2010908624 / ISBN: 978-0-9841356-4-2

Printed in the United States of America
27 26 25 24 23 22 21 20 19 18 17 16 15 14 13 12 11 10 9 8 7 6 5 4 3 2 1

TABLE OF CONTENTS

CHAPTER 1
THE ART OF HOME STAGING AND INTERIOR REDESIGN - 7

- What Are These Diverse Yet Similar Strategies?
- The Purpose of This Book
- The Pictures in This Book
- About the Author
- Why Sellers Need Help
- Why Owners Need Help
- What to Expect

CHAPTER 2
101 CASE STUDIES OF ACTUAL STAGED AND REDESIGNED ROOMS IN RANDOM ORDER BY ASSORTED PROFESSIONAL STAGERS AND REDESIGNERS - 17

- 46 Living Room Case Studies
- 13 Bedroom Case Studies
- 9 Dining Room Case Studies
- 8 Kitchen Case Studies
- 5 Bath Case Studies
- 4 Children Room Case Studies
- 7 Home Office Case Studies
- 3 Shelf Case Studies

- 2 Entry Case Studies
- 1 Hall Case Study
- 1 Reception Room Case Study
- 1 Closet Case Study

CHAPTER 3
LEARNING FROM THE SUCCESS AND FAILURE OF OTHERS - 226

CHAPTER 4
WHERE TO FIND ADDITIONAL TRAINING, VISUAL AIDS, TOOLS AND OTHER RESOURCES - 229

- Courses You Can Take
- Books You Can Acquire
- Best Consultation Aid You'll Find
- Furniture Moving and Lifting Tools
- Design Training by the Author
- Where to Get Resources and Certification
- Testimonials

Do's and Don'ts
in
Home Staging
and Redesign

CHAPTER 1
THE ART OF HOME STAGING AND INTERIOR REDESIGN

What are These Diverse Yet Similar Home Improvement Strategies?

Home staging is the art of preparing a home for sale. It's the art of helping a buyer fall in love with a home and helping them desire to purchase the home. It's the art of romancing the shell (referred to as a house) so that potential buyers can see themselves owning and living in the home – helping buyers see their own furnishings arranged in the home – helping buyers visualize the home's full potential.

On the other hand, interior redesign is the art of helping home owners gain a greater appreciation of their home. It's the art of helping owners appreciate their furnishings in new and more beneficial ways. It's the art of helping owners de-clutter and enhance the home, making it more functional at the same time it is becoming more visually appealing.

Home staging and interior redesign are concepts and philosophies of decorating that are both diverse and similar at the same time. The reason the two concepts are diverse is that home staging includes a high degree of emphasis on depersonalization of the home to make the home look and feel as spacious and neutralized as possible (to avoid distractions from the selling process) and redesign includes a high degree of emphasis on personalization of the home to bring out the owner's full personality and utilization of all of the space to its optimum advantages.

In other words, home staging is a pared down look – a more austere approach to the design and placement of furniture and accessories. It seeks to help buyer's focus on the features and advantages of the house itself, steering clear of anything that would derail that process. Interior redesign, on the other hand, is a full, personality-filled look – an often colorful, stylized approach to the design and placement of furniture and accessories usually already acquired by the owner of the home.

While home staging and interior redesign rely on the exact same rules and concepts when it comes to furniture and accessory arrangement, the goals are vastly different. The goal in staging is to help sell the home for the highest possible price in the shortest amount of time. A stager's work needs to be precise, understated and appealing to a broad segment of potential buyers. Contrastingly, a redesigner seeks to maximize the furnishings the client already owns, helping them to utilize them more effectively and creatively, bringing out their unique personality so the client enjoys living in the home at a higher level and so that the home is organized, more functional and suitable to the lifestyle of the owner in every sense of the word.

The Purpose of This Book

I believe one of the best ways to learn the do's and don'ts of staging and redesign is by studying before and after pictures. By studying the _before_ picture you can train yourself to instantly spot the most glaring problems in how the furniture and accessories have been arranged. Without ever looking at the _after_ picture, a good stager or redesigner should already be formulating solutions in their mind.

Then by having the advantage of seeing the after picture, after another professional had addressed the situation, the stager or redesigner can validate the solutions they had in mind. This is not to say that the solutions one professional uses will be the same as another professional. As a matter of fact, rooms can often be resolved in several different ways, all equally nice. But it is always helpful to study the methods of another professional to determine if you agree with their assessment and solutions or not.

Learning is all about studying what has been done right (so that you can replicate that success) and studying what was done poorly (so that you can avoid those mistakes or at least arrive at solutions that you believe work better). By learning the important concepts professionals use when arranging furniture and accessories, you will discover the creative potential that lies hidden in you and you'll be able to help others reach their goals as well.

The Pictures in This Book

Sometimes readers look at a picture and think that it is dated because the home was built years ago or the furnishings of the client are older furnishings. Please keep in mind as you peruse the Case Studies (purposely given in random order) that these pictures are not dated but the homes or the furniture might be dated giving the *appearance* of having been staged or redesigned a long time ago. I assure you the service itself is not dated.

In the staging and redesign industry, it's not about how old the home may be or how old the furniture may be, but how it ultimately can be re-arranged for the purposes and benefits of the client. We make no value judgments on the clients nor their homes or possessions. Our job is to take what we are given and make it work. Depending on the State and City where the home is located, stagers and redesigners will commonly work on homes that are quite new as well as homes that may be up to 100 years old. Stagers and redesigners will work in all types of styles however the design principles that are applied are applicable to all styles. Some clients will own new furniture; others may own furniture they've had for 30 or more years; some will own antiques. Some homes already on the market may be completely void of any furniture or accessories. How old the furniture is, how dated it may look, is not a concern to the professional re-arranger. What matters is that it is arranged correctly to enhance the home, make the home more accessible and appealing, and make it more enjoyable and useful.

The 101 Case Studies are taken from my vast collection of before and after pictures most submitted by students as part of their certification process, and in almost every case represent their earliest projects when they were brand new in the business. Obviously, then, the work shown will not likely be their best work now but it was their best _early_ work. Because this book is intended to teach all readers how to improve their individual talents, and because the critiques are explicit and critical, I am not disclosing the names of the students. I have even woven into the group examples of some of my own early work, and I've been as hard on myself as I have been on others. You will not know, therefore, whether you're looking at examples of my own work or that of a student. I obviously don't want to embarrass anyone, but I also want you to know that everyone improves with time and experience (even me). I have been mortified to look back on some of my earliest projects as most people would be.

But I'm a firm believer that anyone can be a successful home stager or redesigner and that one of the best possible ways to learn is by studying the examples of work done by others – both excellent or just good – both mediocre or poor. So you will find a mixture of the good, the bad and the ugly in the examples given. In each case, however, I try to point out the initial problems I've noticed in the before picture, clarify what I see was accomplished by the professional stager or redesigner, and then point out tips on how the final outcome might have been strengthened. Where excellent work has been done, I point that out. Where weaker or questionable work has been done, I point that out as well.

By studying the 101 Case Studies and deciding for your self whether each project was managed well or poorly, readers will automatically improve their own assessment skills which, hopefully, will lead to better and better talent to be applied on future projects. So to any of my students reading this book who discover examples of their own work dissected and critiqued within these pages, for better or for worse, please don't be offended or discouraged – I too am critiqued in these pages.

Know that all of the students whose examples are provided in the Case Studies have gone on to succeed in achieving the coveted designation Certified Staging Specialist (CSS) and/or Certified Redesign Specialist (CRS). I am the only trainer in the world who requires candidates to pass an exam (to verify their knowledge) and submit a portfolio (to prove their competence) before awarding them with a designation. Therefore the CSS and CRS designations are highly respected in the industry – they cannot be bought – they have to be earned. Any reader interested in information about these designations will find more information at the end of this book in Chapter 4.

About the Author

I am a Southern California interior redesigner/home staging author and trainer and mentor to tens of thousands. My career in design began in 1972 when I started my own graphic arts and printing business. I staged my first home in 1975, only back then no one called it home staging. In 1983, having tired of the graphic arts business and seeing the handwriting on the wall with the invention of the home computer, I began a successful corporate art consulting career offering home decorating advice here and there for my corporate clients, and providing services in their homes that were separate from my art consulting services. During those years I designed and implemented hundreds of art collections for small, medium, and large businesses, including several Fortune 500 and Fortune 1000 companies. I also wrote and published the popular book of 101 wall grouping designs called, Where There's a Wall -- There's a Way (now sold out but replaced by my book titled Wall Groupings! The Secrets of Arranging Art and Photos).

Since 1986, I have simultaneously served both corporate and residential clients with art and interior redesign and staging services. And in 2002 I began Decorate-Redecorate.Com and offered home study training in staging, redesign and art consulting for tens of thousands of eager entrepreneurs. These entrepreneurs have gone on to create highly successful businesses of their own. Many who have taken my training and courses are also real estate agents. Almost all of them look to me as a personal mentor to help them grow their businesses or expand their services to their clients.

I have written over a dozen books and ebooks (which comprise basic and advanced courses), developed many professional sales and marketing aids, and pulled together highly effective tools to assist in the successful completion of staging and redesign projects.

In addition to that, I have become a published artist. My work has been published in the form of decorative art prints by The McGaw Group of New York and Galaxy of Graphics of New York, though they have sold out and are rare to find these days. Now that you know a bit about me, let's get to work.

Why Sellers Need Help

After decades of staging and rearranging other people's furnishings and visiting homes where my services have not been sought, I have come to the conclusion that most people don't know that their furniture and accessory arrangements are poorly conceived. If they never felt a need for a redesign service all the while they lived in the home, they can't possibly be expected to know now how to make the home attractive for other people when trying to sell it.

If you don't know basic design concepts, you might not know that what you've done (or what you might advise) is ineffective. The most common problems I see are a failure to address a room's natural focal point, failure to create seating arrangements that encourage conversation, failure to balance a room, failure to create a sense of unity, flow and rhythm, huge disparities in sizes, failure to account for proportion and scale, failure to acquire a sufficient amount of accessories, failure to properly assess lighting and failure to maximize traffic lanes.

So what I find over and over again are homes that look and feel chaotic, choppy and totally unappealing. I personally wouldn't want to spend 5 minutes there, much less buy the home.

So while most people do a pretty good job of selecting reasonably nice furniture and accessories (to whatever point they have acquired these things), their sense of placement leaves much to be desired. Therefore their ability to make the home presentable to buyers will leave much to be desired. That's why there is such a need for home staging.

So this is one of the areas you may find to be the biggest challenge - convincing sellers that they have a need that you can dramatically resolve. If you are a realtor® you can learn the benefits and offer authoritative advice to give you a marketing edge over those realtors® who don't.

Why Owners Need Help

In a tough economy people stay in their homes longer. They often build additions to the home because they need more space or because they have family members who need to move back home, or they plan to expand the home and wait for a better time to sell. Regardless of their needs and goals, they are prepared to live there for an indefinite period of time and naturally would like to enjoy the home to the fullest.

That's when the services of a professional interior redesigner (or arranger) become vital. Consumers do a rather good job of purchasing furnishings that are compatible with their lifestyle and color choices. But, unfortunately, they have never learned how to arrange their furnishings in the proper manner to gain the most pleasure and service from their belongings. This is why a professional arranger can easily come in and in a matter of hours transform an ill-conceived furniture arrangement into one that is more useful and more beautiful at the same time. It is not unusual for clients to look with wonder and awe at the transformations that take place almost instantly.

What to Expect in This Guide

In design, it's not just color and style that matter. Placement is crucial to a successful outcome. So with the goal of helping you learn these all important rules and concepts, I decided to bring you a myriad of case studies taken from real situations from all parts of the country so you can learn first hand what doesn't work and why, what does work and why and what could be done better and why.

As you work your way through this manual, you're going to see before pictures of real life situations. I said earlier these are examples I've collected over the years from my own work and from work my students in staging and redesign have submitted to me. As mention previously, so as not to embarrass anyone, I'll not be giving you their names or locations. You'll also see the after pictures so you can see the results. In some cases the results are stunning; in other cases the results were not so stunning, but at least there was some improvement. Where I feel the results were less than optimum, I'll be making comments and suggestions of what steps need to be re-worked, re-positioned or discarded altogether.

As we move through the sequence of examples together, it is my goal that you should be able to sharpen your skills and fine tune your creativity. You will read my comments on choices made by my student that were not the wisest. In every case I'll try to tell you what I told the student in my quest to help them develop their skills.

There are always aspects to arranging furniture and accessories that are more difficult than others and if a student had a misunderstanding of a concept, it often popped up over and over again in their work. You might have the same thing happening in the work you are doing. So if you feel you are more in agreement with what the student did than what I am advising, there are only two ways to view it. 1) Either you are making the same mistakes yourself or 2) You and I will have to agree to disagree. Fair enough?

All I ask of you is to read with an open mind because if you disagree with me, it could just be a matter of personal preference at play. I can assure you that my comments will be based on sound, proven techniques and concepts used universally by interior designers nationwide – so just be open to new ideas if you find yourself in disagreement.

With that said, let's move right into some of our case studies. You're going to see examples taken from expensive homes as well as inexpensive homes. There will be examples from new homes to antiquated homes. There will be new furniture and there will be old furniture – even antiques. There will be homes from all parts of the country. There will be homes representing many different styles.

And while there is a vast difference from one home to another, one thing remains constant. The goal of every stager is to maximize the spaciousness and assets of the home to attract the broadest number of potential buyers. The goal of every redesigner is to maximize for the owner their enjoyment of the home and their furnishings that already exist in the home, giving them a more beautiful environment that is also more functional. The goal for every reader should be to learn from every example so that you enjoy your own home more fully, and if providing a service to clients, you can be the best you can be at what you do.

101

CASE

STUDIES

OF

ACTUAL STAGED

AND REDESIGNED

ROOMS

BY ASSORTED

PROFESSIONALS

CHAPTER 2

Case Study 1

An impressive fireplace commands your attention – at least it wants to. But there are so many conflicting elements all contesting for attention that the eye does not know where to focus first. The single large work of art over the sofa is fine, but then the two ornament stands and the wreath (to the left of the art) create an imbalance on the wall. There are far too many items on the mantle that extends from wall to wall. It looks disorderly and chaotic. So let's see how the professional stager worked to improve the look and feel of the room.

BEFORE

The professional stager cleaned up the space, removing many of the accessories entirely. The large 3-seat leather sofa was replaced by a smaller loveseat and the sofa has been pulled out into the middle of the room. The landscape formatted art on the fireplace was traded for a portrait formatted work of art that mirrors better the shape of the brick above the shelf.

AFTER

A sofa table (or console) has been placed behind the sofa and the family photographs have been neatly arranged on the table. There is more openness against the wall helping to accentuate the twin lamps and end tables flanking the loveseat. A grouping of plates has been hung above the loveseat giving a more contemporary look to the space. The direction of the area rug has been changed as well as the positioning of the coffee table to go along with the repositioning of the sofa.

BARB'S COMMENTS - I think you would agree that the space is more appealing to the eye. I do have a problem with the wall grouping arrangement. It appears to be hung a bit too high over the loveseat and the plate on the far upper right feels out of place, drawing the eye up to the unattractive vents near the ceiling. Since we're looking at the room from an angle, however, it might not look as bad in reality as it appears here. Still, my hunch is that the plate arrangement needs some adjustment to bring it into total balance. I believe the room is still too cluttered. A single large work of art (rather than the plate grouping) would be ideal and the family photographs should have been replaced with accessories of a neutral nature, like ceramics and plants.

BEFORE
This is the opposite side of the same room. You can see the original placement of the loveseat, lots of odds and ends scattered around the room, hats all over the walls and a bit of a mess, to say the least.

In the after shot, notice how clean the window seat has become. The sofa fills the gap making it more of a cohesive unit with the loveseat, now against the wall. The hats are gone, as is the quilt blanket and messiness on the coffee table.

The window treatment has been changed out as well and other items removed from the room. A potential buyer can really get a nice sense of the room and how it can be arranged and yet see the architectural benefits of the room, such as the long window seat.

AFTER

BARB'S COMMENTS: I'm not sure about the substitution of dark drapes for the long bay window. When closed they will darken the room and make it appear smaller. You be the judge. The glass coffee table is much too small for the overstuffed sofa and loveseat and is out of scale. It could have been the only table available. A larger table would have been preferable.

If you have a scale issue of this sort that can't be helped, try to place more accessories on top of the coffee table to give it more visual mass, such as plants or a grouping of accessories.

Case Study 2

BEFORE

The problems with this room are many. Let's start with the most glaring: the placement of the deer heads leads the eye to the ceiling, not into the room. Whatever you may think of deer heads, if you are a redesigner it is not your place to judge your client's selection of accessories.

Having said that, it is paramount that they be appropriately placed on the wall to prevent the room from looking cluttered and messy. There is a TV set on the far left wall and the sofa is unattractively shoved up against the opposite wall with nothing in between to draw the two sides together into a more unified whole. As a matter of fact, all of the furniture in the room is arranged around the perimeter of the room. There is a lot of wasted space in the middle of the room and the overall feeling is one of distance and coldness.

The small old-fashioned frame to the left of the patio doors is much too small for the wall and looks dwarfed in the space. Let's see what our re-arranger did to improve the look and feel of the room.

AFTER
The first thing you'll notice is that the art and the deer heads have been rearranged. The sofa has been pulled out into the middle of the room facing the camera and no doubt the TV has been brought to the far right side of the room so the seating can be focused on the TV. By placing the sofa in the middle of the room perpendicular to the walls, the room now feels wider and not so overly long. There is more unity and a definite improvement here.

BARB'S COMMENTS: The chest serving as a coffee table is much too small in scale for the large sized seating pieces surrounding it. If the recliner is not a wall hugger, its placement will be a problem when anyone wants to recline as it appears overly close to the wall. If it is a wall hugger, however, there is no problem with its placement. There is an imbalance in the pillow arrangement: two dark on the left and two light pillows on the right. Balance the arrangement by putting one dark and one light on each side, or go for a fully asymmetrical arrangement and put the dark pillows on the recliner and the rocking chair, leaving only the light pillows on the sofa. The deer heads and the artwork should be tightened up into a wall grouping that doesn't try to

23

spread from wall to wall. Groupings are best displayed in tight spacing so that the outer shape of the grouping forms a geometric shape and is sized appropriately for the size of the wall. It never works very well to try to spread things out. If this wall had been divided into thirds, and the grouping had been arranged to cover only 2/3^{rds} of the wall, the outcome would have been more cohesive and pleasing to the eye.

BEFORE
Now let's look at the other side of the room. We see the TV on the far right with a charming fireplace on the left of the upper wall. There is a shelf unit and many other smaller pieces. Wall ornamentation is scattered here and there with no rhyme or reason and hung too high at that.

AFTER
As you can see the TV was not only moved to a different wall, it has been placed at an angle in the right corner. By moving the TV as close to the fireplace as possible, the redesigner has been able to arrange the seating so that the family can enjoy a nice fire in the fireplace while watching TV. This is the ideal type of arrangement.

BARB'S COMMENTS: The room does indeed look much better than before. The seating is more conducive to real enjoyment of the room. There are still many accessories in the room, and some are still hung too high and in random places, but the redesigner was able to achieve maximum usage of the room. She retained much of what was in the room but made it more functional and pleasing to the eye. Other than the scale issue mentioned earlier with the coffee table and some remaining random issues with the placement of wall ornamentation, this room is perhaps as good as it can get under the circumstances. The whole goal of a redesigner is to work with what the client already has and achieve a more beautiful and functional room without spending any money, so please don't let that goal escape your thoughts. If the goal was to stage this room to sell the house, there needs to be more editing of the furniture and accessories.

Case Study 3

BEFORE

At first glance, the arrangement of this room doesn't appear to be all the bad. The owner clearly has arranged the seating to face what appears to be an entertainment center.
However, the art, lamp and floral arrangement sitting on top of the unit feel out of balance and could use some improvement. The artwork feels a bit too small to be in good scale with the furniture below, and while the lamp and floral help to change the visual scale, it really isn't working all that well. So let's see what kind of creativity the professional arranger gave to this room.

AFTER
Two smaller vertically formatted images were hung side by side to create better scale with the entertainment center. To open up the traffic lanes and give a more creative arrangement to the seating, the professional arranger has angled the seating, balancing the sofa on one side with two matching chairs on the opposite side.

BEFORE

On the right wall to the left is a large console in a contemporary style with a large framed mirror above. The two skinny traditional lamps are under scale and really don't improve the situation.

Other accessories sitting on the glass top appear to be adding to a cluttered outcome.

AFTER

The professional arranger removed the two lamps, added a larger floral on one end and just tidied up the whole arrangement. This contemporary room now feels a whole lot more spacious and inviting. The angled furniture arrangement is pleasing to the eye and an unexpected treatment which brings an element of surprise to the room.

BARB'S COMMENTS: I'm not sure what is going on with the angled area rug behind the seating arrangement. In this shot there appears to be another chair on the opposite side of the room. Not being able to see everything there is to see, I'm uncomfortable with the area rug, but all else appears to be pleasing to the eye and there are plenty of ways the owners can enter the room and enjoy it to the fullest.

Case Study 4

BEFORE
This empty bathroom belongs to a home to be sold. Naturally any home stands a better chance of selling if there is some decorating in the space. So our professional stager added just enough decorative treatments to give the room some extra romance. Let's look at her solution.

AFTER
The stager added a couple of small plants, a taller vase and some reeds at the far end where the mirror had ended and you can see a wall ornament on the opposite wall reflected in the mirror. While we can't see the other sink in this shot, I'm quite certain a plant was also added to that area as well.

BARB'S COMMENTS: There is a definite improvement in the way this bathroom shows now. Perhaps some towels laid on the bathtub would have completed the look. The wall ornament could have been hung lower so one's attention is not drawn to the large blank space between the base of the ornament and the top of the tub which would be magnified when one sits in the tub. Other than that, I think the stager did an excellent job in this bathroom.

Case Study 5

BEFORE
Well, we have some serious problems here. First we have two rows of shelves that extend almost from the door to the wall, leaving very little wall space to "frame" the shelves. So right off the bat, they look a bit crowded. To make matters worse, we've got a very small console table beneath the shelves, which only accentuates the heaviness above, making the shelving treatment feel very oppressive. We've got gaping "holes" on each side of the table below, drawing the eye rather to the holes instead of the furnishings. So let's see if our rearranger was able to solve this truly unfortunate method of decorating.

AFTER
While the rearranger (redesigner) did make an improvement, let's first discuss the effective improvements. First, the design element between the shelves was enlarged and literally creates a focal point in the middle, giving the eye a place to focus first. This is a good thing.

Next, the accessories on the shelves have been changed and the re-arranger brought in some candles to create some height changes and made the shelves look less cluttered and more unified. This also is a good thing. Then she exchanged the smaller table beneath for a wider table and reduced the number of accessories on it to three and added a little bit of height to visually bring the shelves and the table closer together. This is a good thing.

BARB'S COMMENTS: But we still have some serious gaps on the sides of the tables which still make the shelving section feel top heavy and oppressive. The eye is still drawn to the blank space on each side and the small basket beneath the table is under scale for that space as well. It would have been nice if two matching floor plants had been placed on each side of the table to fill the spaces. By placing taller plants that match, the re-arranger would have helped to unify all of the elements together into one complete whole and would have increased the visual weight along the bottom so that the shelves would no longer have felt too heavy above. If plants did not already exist in the home, it certainly should have been put on a shopping list.

Case Study 6

BEFORE
This playroom needs serious help. The client set everything up along the perimeter of the room. While no one really expects great things out of a playroom, it doesn't have to look junky and out of control. This room has no personality and does not invite anyone inside to appreciate it in any way. So let's see what the redesigner did with this room.

AFTER
Wow! What a difference! What an improvement. The redesigner added some family photographs which appear to be blowups mounted in or on Lucite boxes. The words "a family that plays together stays together" has been artfully added above the pictures, which are hung above the sofa. The pillows on the sofa are more artfully arranged and some appear to be newer and larger and hopefully repeat the colors of the photographs on the wall. The bare windows now have a window treatment. Many of the toys have been removed or stored elsewhere in the room.

This is an excellent example of simple yet creative touches and rearrangement services at work. The outcome is stunning.

BEFORE
This is a view of the side of the room near the sofa. As you can see the proportions of the shelf units are all wrong for

the size of the wall. One's attention is drawn yet again to all that blank space above the toys.

AFTER
The redesigner brilliantly brought in some taller shelf units and a table to serve as a desk with matching chairs to improve the proportions. Now the space has added functionality as well as eye appeal. It is a room small children can enjoy as well as older children and adults.

BARB'S COMMENTS: I would still like to see the photographs hung a little lower over the sofa, but other than that, I feel the redesigner did an excellent job in turning this previously bland playroom into an attractive space for the adults as well as young kids or teenagers. Well done!

Case Study 7

BEFORE
This kitchen is almost ready to be shown to prospective buyers but it still leaves one a little cold. Yes, it's good to create a neutral environment with uncluttered counters but there needs to be a little bit of romance added here to improve the chances of helping buyers fall in love with this kitchen.

AFTER
So let's see what the professional stager did to improve the look and feel of this slightly bland kitchen. First of all she edited out many of the pottery and vases and bottles from the shelf unit. She removed the unsightly towels and rags from the sink area. She added a lovely floral arrangement to the window sill, drawing one's attention to the outside.

Then she cleverly created simple place settings on the island with a centerpiece that easily suggests this area as a handy place to grab a bite to eat.

Sometimes staging strategies are simple and perhaps even hardly noticeable. But what a beautiful difference they can make. Notice the cookbook on the counter near the stove. No flatware is added to the place settings for security reasons. One of the bar stools has been removed creating a more open and spacious feeling.

BARB'S COMMENTS: I think the stager did an outstanding job of taking this otherwise unexciting kitchen and giving it just the right amount of pizzazz. It makes you want to cook and eat here – and that's the whole point, right?

Case Study 8

BEFORE
No need to tell you this isn't working very well. It appears to be a largely empty room with these plants shoved to one corner and perhaps waiting for someone to re-arrange them. I believe that's an ottoman in the foreground. So I'm excited to see what the professional stager did in this situation.

AFTER
Ahh, I'm greatly relieved. The stager brought in a large wicker set comprised of 2 matching chairs, a settee and a coffee table. It appears from this angle that the seating arrangement was also angled when compared with the fireplace. This is especially interesting when you note that the flooring is a grid design, making the angle or the furniture just that much more noticeable. It does look nice in the picture. The stager also added some refreshments on the table, further creating a lovely, relaxed atmosphere for buyers to appreciate.

BARB'S COMMENTS: It's difficult to tell from this photo whether the angled arrangement vs. the grid pattern of the floor work optimally. It might have worked better to go with the grid and place the furniture at the same angle as the grid pattern, but honestly I would have to be in the room to fully judge that. I would like to have seen some type of art or ornamentation above the fireplace as the wall looks very, very bare. But at least the space appears lovely and perhaps the angled furniture arrangement helps to draw the eye outside to what appears to be a nice garden area. Overall I think this staging is very effective. With the large windows left bare, the room appears to be a beautiful "garden room" and is very inviting to the eye.

Case Study 9

BEFORE
Busy wallpaper in a small bathroom is always a problem. It can make one feel a bit dizzy and it makes it more difficult to appreciate any accessories in the room. The large number of

Bathroom2Before

utilitarian items on the counter make for an unappealing space. A person might live this way but it's no way to try to sell a home, that's for sure.

AFTER
So let's now take a look at what the stager/redesigner did with this room. Obviously the busy wallpaper was not removed. However, accessories of a higher contrast in color were brought in, which clearly command attention. The wallpaper fades properly into the background as the accessories move to center stage. The ugly bottles and jars and toothbrush have been removed or at least stored out of sight. What an improvement!!

Bathroom2After

BARB'S COMMENTS: I'm not fond of the position of the picture hung off to the left of the small towel rod on the wall. The towel hanger should have been removed and the picture should have been centered above the sink counter so there would not be an imbalance. The towel hanger could have been easily placed in another location. The addition of the soap dispenser on the right side of the sink is a good idea. I think I would not have put the two smaller items on the sink next to the tall lamp. I'm not sure what they add and doubt if they are needed. Since they are not in good scale with the lamp, they hurt the final outcome of the design. When dealing with busy wall paper, it is essential to pick accessories in high color contrast so that they stand out more than the wall paper. Wall paper, no matter how pretty, should not overtake the furnishings and accessories.

Case Study 10

BEFORE
First and foremost, the overly small picture (which is totally out of scale for this bed) is hung way, way too high. This not only pulls the attention away from the bed and toward the ceiling, but the eye is drawn to the gaping hole between the two. Not good. Not good at all. The bed itself leaves something to be desired. The arrangement on the night stand seems overly cluttered and some editing is needed. So let's see what the stager did here.

Bedroom3Before

AFTER

Much, much better. Narrow beds will look much wider if you create strong horizontal lines that go from one side of the bed to the other side, such as the stager did here with the dark blanket. She repeated this horizontal line by folding back the quilt at the top of the bed. Then she stacked the pillows at an angle to bring in some height. That is not a mirror above the bed; it is some kind of abstract art. Were it not for the dark blanket at the foot of the bed, it would probably feel too heavy and too large for the bed, but as it is, I think the stager can get away with it. Notice the bedside table arrangement has been simplified.

Bedroom3After

BARB'S COMMENTS: It's unfortunate that the headboard appears to be too big for the box springs and mattress. This would not be so noticeable if the quilt were not folded back as it is. So the stager had to make a choice here. What do you think?

Case Study 11

BEFORE
One of the curious things to me is the tendency on the part of home owners to try to "fill" the space up by spreading things out. Case in point. We've got two sconces on the wall, clearly placed beyond the width of the dresser below. So the owner placed two pictures between them and it appears they spread the pictures equal distance from each other and equal distance from the sconces. Not good. This makes the arrangement noticeably thin, and it makes it appear top heavy as well. There is also this awkward gap between the base of the art and the accessories on the dresser. To make matters worse, we've got this awkward picture on the right wall, with another small table in the corner. The penguins (an obvious collection) are broken up and sprinkled in random places in the room, making everything look very cluttered and unorganized.

Bedroom1 Before

So let's see if the redesigner made any improvement to the room.

AFTER

Bedroom1 After

Why yes! I believe we see a major improvement here. The sconces have been swapped for different ones. One of the pictures has been removed and the sconces and picture are tightly arranged. Care has been taken not to exceed the width of the dresser, which places the arrangement in good scale and keeps the visual weight on the bottom where it belongs. Three of the penguins have been grouped together drawing special attention to them. All of the rest of the stuff has been removed or placed elsewhere in the home. The picture on the right wall has been replaced with a long vertical wall ornament that replicates the shape of the narrow panel of wall next to the window. The space is now serene and inviting. K to the stager who solved the very obvious problems this room had before.

Case Study 12

BEFORE

It's quite common for many home owners and sellers to use the refrigerator as a place to park magnets, notes, reminders, family photos and a wide variety of items for daily use. The sofa appears to be backed up against the kitchen counter, but that's the problem with photographs – they can't show depth. I'm sure there's a traffic lane between the two. There is a small dinette on the left side of the kitchen. The main problem here is an issue of clutter – lots of clutter.

Now let's see what the stager was able to achieve.

AFTER

Gone are all the magnets. Gone are all the notes, reminders and photos from the refrigerator. A major improvement right there! The dinette has been replaced with a more luxurious dining table and upholstered chairs. A small floral arrangement is on the table which helps make the area look more charming. Two place settings were also added to the table as a further enhancement treatment. All of the utilitarian items have been removed from the counters. A console has been placed beneath the counter and against the half wall. The kitchen appears spotless and the sofa moved. Fabulous!

BARB'S COMMENTS: I love what was done in the kitchen and dining room. It totally works! The space looks white glove clean and very inviting. I'm hesitant about the console (table) in the foreground. I don't understand why the stager put it there. Perhaps it was to remove the large amount of white wall in an otherwise dark area. It's always good if there is a practical reason for doing something like this. I can't exactly think of one, so my recommendation would be to remove the console altogether.

Case Study 13

BEFORE

This is one of those really difficult rooms. Due to the configuration of the door and windows, the size of the room and the owner's furnishings, there is one major problem with the way it is currently arranged. It's what we call "screaming distance". There is a large screen wall mounted TV on the left wall, just out of view. The distance between the TV and the sectional is huge – they are much further apart than recommended. It creates a vast divide and anyone entering or leaving the room must cross between the TV and the seating area. The narrow runner (rug) on the floor is helpful in protecting the carpet from dirt and debris, but it acts as a clear, visual divide and is not appealing and also out of scale. Apart from changing out the furniture completely, there is a limited amount of improvement that can be made in this room. But let's see what the re-arranger did.

AFTER

The runner has been removed. The table has been cleared off, a centerpiece of candles added and the chairs have been rearranged in a manner that brings more perceived unity to the room. Some of the sectional has been removed, as well as an end table, reducing the amount of furniture and making the room feel more spacious. Unfortunately the "screaming distance" between the sectional and the TV, looking like the TV is in a hall. Items on the ottoman have been reduced as well.

BARB'S COMMENTS: Sometimes it's impossible to remove all of the problems in a room. Here is one situation in which the size and configuration of the room doesn't allow for many options, though the TV should have been relocated. But I think you'll agree that a major improvement was made by the stager and the room looks very appealing and far more spacious than before.

Case Study 14

BEFORE

Foyers or entry ways are very important to a home whether it is being staged or redesigned. That's because the entry sets the stage for the rest of the home. This area is often ignored by owners or sellers, yet it is necessary to pay great attention to the look and feeling of the entry of any home.

In this situation, we have a large floral print, nicely framed and a lovely antique table with marble top placed in the corner with a plant on the other side. Because the spacing of these 3 major elements is pretty wide, the entry does not look attractive and cohesive.

Foyer #1 - Before

AFTER

The re-arranger decided to replace the art. This was a good decision because the previous floral was not strong enough to be appropriate for such an important spot. A beautiful garden scene seems a perfect choice. The antique table has been pulled out from the corner and closer to the middle of the wall. It has also been nicely balance by two floor plants instead of one. Since the 3 major elements are now situated closer together, they act as one unit instead of 3 separate units. This is good design.

Foyer #1 - After

BARB'S COMMENTS: Removing excess bare wall in the middle of a grouping of furniture or accessories is important. The attention of the viewer should not be drawn to the bare wall (negative space). When you place furniture and accessories in groupings, stand back and see where your eye is drawn. Make sure you place pieces close together. Most people are too spacious in their placement when they should tighten up the placement grouping (or vignette).

Case Study 15

BEFORE
At first glance you would not think there was anything wrong with this room. It actually looks quite nice, however there is no WOW factor. So to help this room stand out more, the

Guest Bedroom #1 - Before

stager decided to make just a few simple changes that really made an immediate impact. The long lines of the quilted comforter make the bed look long and very narrow.

AFTER
A picture on the wall above the bed helps create different levels in the room for more interest. Adding the tree brings an element of life into the room and helps create a comfortable step down in the height of the art compared to other elements in the room. The layering of multiple pillows on the bed brings out a far more luscious, luxurious feeling. The folded blanket at the foot of the bed helps make the bed feel much wider. The room is charming and very feminine.

Guest Bedroom #1 - After

BARB'S COMMENTS This is clearly a woman's room but it also conjures up thoughts of a great guest bedroom. The choice of artwork feels a bit dark and a little oppressive but I like the added height and the personality that has been brought out in the room. Well done overall.

Case Study 16

BEFORE
Book shelves are always tricky for many people. They can quite easily be overstuffed with mismatched items, brimming full and looking quite messy and unappealing. Here the owner did a good job of selecting items that fill the height of each shelf, not just its width. Usually the height of each shelf compartment is ignored. But there is just too much going on here to be visually appealing and let's see how our redesigner tackled this issue.

AFTER
First it is apparent that many of the books have been edited out and placed elsewhere or stored. Items of like kind have been grouped together (i.e. the sail boats bottom left have been put in the same compartment). This helps draw the eye to them and the larger of the two stands in the back with the smaller boat layered in front. Nicely done. Care has also

been taken to help balance the entire bookshelf through the use of color distribution. Notice how the light colors are sprinkled throughout the case, as are the darker and medium colors. Color is a great way to control balance.

After - Merida Great Room

Compartments with books are usually filled just with books. This helps to lessen the cluttered look and bring some unity to the room.

BARB'S COMMENTS: The large art on top with the tall baskets is an asymmetrical placement. Since I cannot see the whole wall, I don't know if this addition makes the arrangement too tall or not, but I do know it is an A-line wall, sloping down from left to right. One needs to be careful how high up the wall one goes. I've seen pictures of the other parts of this room but I can't include them because they are quite blurred. Needless to say, the re-arranger had an uphill battle to fight in a room that was over the top in terms of the amount of furnishings. So all in all, I felt the redesigner did make a significant contribution to improving the overall look and feel of the room, though I feel more editing would have been advantageous.

Case Study 17

BEFORE
This uneventful office leaves visitors feeling a bit uneasy. The floor plant and the ceramic fish are out of proportion to the area and look a bit helter-skelter. The phone cord hanging down makes it look even worse. So let's see how this reception room came alive with unexpected design.

Reception Before

AFTER
The redesigner noted the lack of good scale and proportion against the far wall and set about to make some nice improvements. She added artwork about koi fish on the wall to bring the design up to eye level. By adding more plants and creating a large grouping with the ceramic fish, the entire corner of this waiting area came alive.

Reception After

BARB'S COMMENTS: A great way to change scale or proportion is by adding more elements together into a tightly arranged grouping. It was essential to include the artwork on the wall for the height it brought and then let each piece gradually reduce the height down to the floor. So notice that the highest point is the artwork, then about ½ way down you'll see the fronds of the fern sitting on the small table or bench. Further down are the other two plants, and the lowest points are defined by the ceramic fish. It makes for an interesting corner and really helps give this reception room some personality. Well done!

Case Study 18

BEFORE
This dining room is a blank canvass to a home stager. It is dark, empty, cold and uninviting. The long shadows of the trees make it feel lonely and a bit depressing. How would this appeal to a potential buyer coming through the home? I would venture to say it would be a tough sell.

AFTER
Drawing from the stager's inventory of furnishings, here is the charming result she was able to achieve for her client. This stager began with a bold area rug to really make a strong statement in the room. It anchors the table beautifully because it is larger than the table. To be effective, an area rug much be sufficiently larger than the table and all of the chairs should sit on the rug with plenty of room to pull the chair out from the table for seating someone. The rug must serve not

only as a decorative addition, but it must <u>frame</u> the furniture sufficiently to be in <u>proper scale</u>.

Next the table choice is the perfect size and format for this rectangular room. The strong color of the table contrasts nicely with the wall color. Each of the four chairs have been nicely appointed with a table setting with coordinating colors. A couple of nesting tables are placed in the left corner to finish the room in an exquisite manner.

BARB'S COMMENTS: I'm not sure why the tall branch-like stalk was place in the far right corner - perhaps to conceal the white switch plate on the wall? I don't think it is needed, so I would have eliminated that from the room. Kudos to the stager anyway.

Case Study 19

BEFORE

In this same house as Case Study 18, we find the large living room with a massive white fireplace mantel. We've got massive walls and massive windows. This room will require a substantial amount of large pieces to be in good proportion with the size of the room. It's a challenge but let's see if our stager is up to the task.

AFTER

Yes, she is certainly up to the challenge! She began with a large, dramatic Oriental area rug which looks exquisite against the high polished wood floors. Her next excellent choice was a fully upholstered sofa and two matching lounge chairs. The size of these pieces is appropriate for the room. Since buyers will walk into the room and see the back of the sofa in it's chosen position, she countered this with a nice sofa table (console). On the sofa table, she placed various large accessories to add some height to this part of the room as well. A tall curio cabinet was placed along the far wall, with other pieces nearby for balance and scale. A single tall floral arrangement was placed on the mantel which extends about 2/3rds the height of the white surround, thus drawing one's attention to the room's natural focal point. The use of a free standing folding room divider and a tree on the opposite side of the fireplace add extra interest and perhaps block a view that might not be all that attractive.

BARB'S COMMENTS: Perhaps the room divider and tree are placed there to diminish the huge drop in height from the very top of the crown molding. The visual drop would have been much greater if looking from the crown down to the top of the two lounge chairs. I wonder what it would have looked like, however, to leave an unobstructed view out the windows. Under the circumstances, however, I think the stager did an admirable job in pulling this room together so the house could go on the market and attract some offers.

Case Study 20

BEFORE
This great room leaves much to be desired. Almost all of the furniture is sprinkled around the perimeter of the room, as if

one is trying to fool people into believing it is fully furnished. But the opposite feeling is generated. It looks unfinished. It looks as if it is neglected. It looks and feels uncomfortable. It just doesn't work at all.

AFTER
In stark contrast, the work of this exceptional redesigner made all the difference in the world and took a very unattractive room and gave it a fabulous new look. By utilizing the center of the room, and not just the perimeter, the room is welcoming; it feels complete and finished; it expresses a strong personality and it looks planned.

A new area rug was brought in to anchor the seating arrangement. A different sofa, with two coordinating occasional chairs facing the sofa, completes the main seating arrangement. The bench, which had been originally placed under the window at the far end, is brought over against the left wall. A beautiful grouping consisting of a large work of art flanked by two sconces holding vases make a dramatic statement while adding some height to balance with the other walls in the room. You can hardly see it, but a 3rd seating arrangement has been incorporated in front of the window, which sports a new window treatment. A buffet or lowboy completes the room on the right side, and along with a tree, helps to balance the overall presentation. What a huge improvement this design turned out to be.

BARB'S COMMENTS: While I can't see everything there is to see in this room in this one picture, I'm delighted with the creativity and thoughtful placement of everything. This redesigner has great talent and has mastered her craft well. I'm not a fan of chairs or sofas sitting partly on an area rug and partly off, however, so for that reason I can't give 100% praise in this situation, but that's a minor point and for many it's also a personal preference.

Case Study 21

BEFORE
We have another empty room. Sometimes there isn't enough furniture available to stage every room in a house to be sold. So a stager must pick and choose the more important places to concentrate on first.

AFTER
In this case the stager decided to decorate this room with a vignette – just a smaller grouping of furniture to suggest a practical usage of the room, give it some decorative treatment, but make no attempt to fully decorate the room. It is an effective strategy and better than leaving the room totally empty. As you can see the large chaise, chest of drawers and tree pull you into the room visually. The wooded yard behind is a nice backdrop for this room. A potential buyer could easily see this as a nice sitting room to read, as a guest room or as a hobby room. Being able to silently give buyers different options for a room's usage is always

welcome and encouraged and a benefit to the seller when done correctly.

BARB'S COMMENTS: I have no complaints about the way this room was staged. I think it was cleverly done and while the pieces are large, the room still feels spacious. When a room is rather small and the pieces are large, it's vital to keep the furnishings to a minimum. Staged homes should always look as spacious as possible.

Case Study 22

BEFORE
Here we have the A-line pitched roof with a large window on the left. The room is empty and crying out for something of beauty. How would you stage a room like this? Before you look at the after picture, study the room's architecture and think about it for awhile. Then look and see what this stager did to make this room come alive.

AFTER
The obvious choice was to turn the room into a bedroom. Since the ceilings are high, a tall headboard was selected to help fill the space and is an excellent choice. Two matching night stands flank the bed and two matching lamps were placed on each. This type of repetition is common, especially in more traditional styles. The stager even used two companion reproductions on the wall, framed the same way. A low dresser was also brought in to help balance the room.

More could have been done to this room, but remember we're staging it to help the house sell, so one always has to be careful about how full the room should become. The entire room, including the bedding, is neutral in color so there is nothing here that would turn a buyer off when it comes to color. It is actually a well staged room.

BARB'S COMMENTS: The choices for this room work for me, however, the two night stands are placed too far from the bed. Again this is one of the problems I see repeated often by students, sellers and owners. They want to take the available space, split it in half and place pieces right in the middle of the available space. Don't do this. The bed and the night stands need to be a grouping of 3. By moving the night stands closer to the bed, you help them <u>feel</u> like a united <u>whole</u> instead of 3 independent objects placed to <u>fill</u> the available space. There should be more space framing the grouping on the outside than within the grouping itself. By moving the night stands closer to the bed than they are from the outer walls, this would have been a winning combination.

Case Study 23

BEFORE

When there are several rooms in a home to be staged, and some of them are similar in size, it's advantageous to show multiple usages for the room in a home. You never know what criteria a potential buyer has, so the more ideas you can give them as they walk through the home, the better. In the previous Case Study, the stager selected a bedroom idea for buyers to see. Let's see what she chose for this empty room with low ceilings.

AFTER

If you guessed a home office, you were correct. This is the perfect type of room to turn into an office. But it doesn't have to be completely outfitted as an office in order to carry the idea across to a buyer.

A large dramatic desk has been brought in with a decorative chair. It looks more like a dining room chair than an office chair, but sometimes you just have to work with what you have. A large chair is placed in the opposite corner for balance, along with a small floor lamp. To finish the sparsely decorated room, an intricate wall decoration is hung. No window treatment has been added and buyers are pulled into the room and encouraged to view the back yard with no obstructions.

BARB'S COMMENTS: I love the desk and how dramatically it pulls you into the room. I'm not sure about the artwork on the stand in the corner, however. I think it may just be a bit distracting. You know, if it's not truly needed, don't clutter up the room when staging it. The other problem is that the top of the art stand should be higher so that there isn't as drastic a height change from the top of the window down to the stand. This creates a <u>cliff-like effect</u> which is not that appealing to the eye.

Case Study 24

BEFORE

Isn't this the way we often live? The table becomes a catch-all for everything. Pictures get put up on the wall in random places with no rhyme or reason. Stuff gets put here and there. We accumulate and accumulate and are lucky if it makes its way into the garage, basement, attic or storage. We're afraid to discard anything because we think we might regret it in the future. Then we expect other people to come into our cluttered nightmare and appreciate our living environment – and maybe even want to purchase it. So we need to be reminded that we must not try to sell a house the way we tend to live in one. We've got a number of problems with this dining room. We can see at least 6 pictures on the wall in a small amount of space. Below the pictures is a busy wallpaper border, followed by a chair rail, followed by a different kind of wallpaper. We have a table that looks almost like a ping pong table, several chairs around the table, then more chairs pushed up against the wall. I have no idea what's hanging from the chandelier. This stager has her work cut out for her.

detailed

AFTER
What a difference! The upper wallpaper has been removed and the wall painted. The artwork has been significantly reduced, the mess cleared from the table, and the chairs reduced to just four around the table. Gone is whatever was hanging from the chandelier. A major improvement to say the least.

BARB'S COMMENTS: The scale of the two smaller pictures flanking the large one is off and the colors too divergent, making the grouping weak. I'm not clear on the white sheer fabric draped in and around the darker fabric on the window. A larger centerpiece and table settings for all 4 chairs would be nice; the walls look great.

Case Study 25

BEFORE
The built-ins really overtake the fireplace in spite of the mirror above the surround. This empty room needs the attention of a professional stager to make it come alive. While it has nice features, it needs some romancing.

AFTER
The stager didn't try to fill up all the shelves. She just brought in a few pieces and placed on the shelves to draw attention to the shelves and suggest to potential buyers that there was plenty of space available. She brought in a large lounge chair with ottoman, placed an open book on the ottoman along with some pillows on the chair. As you can see, you can get away with very little if need be. I would have liked to see her do more with the room, but I don't know what the circumstances were.

detailed

BARB'S COMMENTS: I would have liked to see the wall between the storage units at the bottom and the shelves painted white to draw less attention to that part of the room. This would have helped to center the attention on the fireplace in the middle of the room, rather than to what surrounds the fireplace. I would have liked to see greater attention given to balancing the left side of the room with the right side of the room. It should not have been too difficult to place a few more accessories or books on the shelves – or even some plants. I don't think the stager took this room far enough in the staging process and a little more attention would have made a world of difference. But it was a step in the right direction.

Case Study 26

BEFORE

Great rooms can be difficult to arrange, particularly if they are long and narrow spaces. Here we see the owner separated the room into 3 distinctly different sections: a dining area, a living room area with fireplace, and a TV viewing area. The idea was good but the execution was poor.

AFTER
The tile floor has been replaced by a beautiful hardwood floor. The direction of the planks helps to make the room appear wider. This was a good decision. The large area rug has been replaced by a smaller rug between the sofas. The dining room has moved into the foreground and the former dining room has now become the piano room. Two matching sofas have been brought in and placed facing each other. A sofa table has been placed behind one of the sofas and one of the two lounge chairs has closed off the seating area. The table and chairs have been brought to the other side of the room.

BARB'S COMMENTS: The scale of the three works of art on the back wall is much improved over the three in the first photo. However, they would work better if the three pieces were hung closer together as a unit of one. This would also keep the arrangement from looking spaced out and the far right piece from hanging too close to the light switch by the door on the right. In addition, the vases on the fireplace shelf are too small in scale when compared to the artwork. They are also placed too close to the outer sides of the shelf on both sides. Always make sure you place accessories roughly 1/3rd the way in from the side of the shelf. It makes them feel more comfortable on the shelf and eliminates fear they are about to fall off. The tables chosen for behind the white sofa appear too wide and I think they are probably end tables. Since the tables appear to be black, they draw too much attention and I'd rather see an actual sofa table there instead. Still in all, the changes made by the redesigner here were substantial and much improved the look of the room. The dark arm chair does tend to visually stick out too much, however.

Case Study 27

BEFORE

The proverbial empty kitchen has little to no personality. The only visible evidence someone once lived here is the border print above the upper cabinets. Yes, it looks very clean and move-in ready, but it's also dated. So now let's see if a home stager can actually make it look charming to tempt some buyers.

AFTER
Well, this kitchen didn't just get a pick-me-up, it got a whole face lift. Basically this is outside the scope of this manual, but I thought the results to be too outstanding to eliminate it as a case study. New cabinets (expanded and taller) were brought in, the counters got new granite tops, we're looking at a new stove, new overhead pot lights and a whole new updated look. Beautiful. Notice the lights below the upper cabinets, the addition of a wine holder, and the window

treatment. Then there are the accessories to pull in all the finishing touches for a grand upgrade. Well done!

BARB'S COMMENTS: Depending on your comfort level, you may or may not wish to tackle a complete upgrade of a kitchen. Accessories and a window treatment would have helped the original kitchen quite a bit, but don't you just love an upgrade? If you're doing staging and redesign as a business and don't have the skills or training to do something like this, you can always partner with 3rd party companies to do what needs to be done. So you can take your business in any direction you choose and get as involved as you wish.

Case Study 28

Haven't you been here before? Everyone hurried off to work and school, and left the placemats on the table looking bored to the hilt. A too small plant sits in the middle of the table and a very lonely out of proportion painting is stuck up on the shelf formed by the tops of the cabinets. Maybe it was painted by a daughter or son, but by itself it looks so out of place. The counters are cleared to a degree but there are notes stuck on the refrigerator and it just doesn't look very inviting.

AFTER
If you've got space above the cabinets in your kitchen or your client's kitchen, take advantage of this space and decorate it fully. It won't make the kitchen look smaller and it will be a

feature that prospective buyers will like about the kitchen. See what a difference this stager made using mostly plants and a few other accessories. She then added a larger floral arrangement to the table and put another arrangement on the island, cleared away some of the utilitarian items from the counters and replaced them with more decorative items.

BARB'S COMMENTS: If you elect not to put any plates on the placemats, then remove them. It cuts down on the cluttered look. The plants on the shelf are great but the heights are weak. Seek to fill the vertical height between the shelf and the ceiling up to 2/3rds the available space. Overall the stager made an improvement here, but it could have been tightened up and improved upon. The area rug below the table should be larger. When you pull the chairs back to sit down, you would be half on the rug and half off.

Case Study 29

BEFORE
The most glaring problems here lie with the fireplace wall.
The good thing is that the owner placed the TV as close to the
fireplace as possible, at an angle in the left upper corner. The
seating is arranged so that the owners can enjoy watching TV
at the same time they enjoy a lovely fire crackling nearby.
But that's about all I can say for this room that is positive.
We've got sconces off to the side on both sides of the
fireplace, and electrical outlets that are a contrasting color to
the wall, making them jump out in view. The candles on the
mantel are way under scale.

AFTER
Thankfully the redesigner removed the candles from the
mantel and replaced them with matching vases with some
reeds, in better scale with the picture, which has been
lowered. A sofa table has been placed behind the sofa which

breaks the barrier of the sofa's back and adds interest and surprise to this part of the room. More wall decoration has been added behind the recliners to the right. There are other changes too, but one really can't see everything. The grouping of 3 vases sitting on the tile (in front of the fireplace) help to draw the attention away from the electrical plugs.

BARB'S COMMENTS: The plates on the electrical outlets should have been switched out for ones that come as close as possible to the wall color so they virtually disappear from view. If you can't replace the plates, cover them with matching wallpaper or paint them – anything to make them visually go away. Failing that, paint the wall white again!!! It appears the sofa may sit a bit too far away from the TV and fireplace. Watch out for screaming distance.

Case Study 30

BEFORE

Besides the messiness, this kitchen also lacks what is needed to make it feel beautiful, functional and an enticing place to cook a meal. There are places, albeit small places, to add some interest and charm. The first job, however, is to get rid of the mess.

AFTER
Take a look at how the re-arranger brought in some plants and accessories to fill up the space above the top cabinets. The counters are cleaned off and only decorative items appear. An island has been moved in by bringing in a low boy from another room. Clever! A large round area rug anchors the dining room set and is amply large to accommodate the chairs when pulled away from the table.

BARB'S COMMENTS: The improvement to this kitchen is stunning, simple and nicely done. The room to the left looks like it needs some professional intervention, but the kitchen and dinette area are much improved. Selected accessories have been included on the counters, but not overdone.

Case Study 31

BEFORE
Little girls! Don't ya just love 'em? But can't they be messy?
But seriously, boy or girl, children tend to be naturally
disorganized and their rooms are often a disaster area. So
what's a mother (or seller) to do? A real challenge for one
professional stager, let's see what got accomplished.

AFTER
Now what could be better? The stager did a marvelous job of
organizing this room, adding plastic storage bins under the
bed and making everything easily accessible for the child.

BARB'S COMMENTS: Some artwork hung on the wall above the shelf compartments would have helped to make the room look more complete and could have also drawn away some of the focus from the busyness of the toys and books, making the room settle down a bit. Oh, if only it could stay like this though!

Case Study 32

BEFORE

It's not unusual for people to live with accessories placed all over a room in a random manner with little to no thought at all about good placement design. This is usually because they don't know any better or things get added to a wall at spaced intervals because they just bought something or were given something and they wanted to display it. While people may choose to live this way, it's no way to sell a home. So let's see what our professional staging student did with this room while working to complete her certification requirements.

AFTER
As you can see, everything was taken down from the wall except for the clock, which was moved and centered off the table and lowered to a more appropriate height at eye level. The kitchen has been stripped bare of all clutter and utilitarian appliances. I can still see the lowest picture on the

wall just to the right of the window. I'm hoping that all four of these pictures were removed, but I have a hunch they weren't. Still the space is much more suitable to welcome potential buyers and generate some offers.

BARB'S COMMENTS: I think more could have been done to this space to make it look enticing. For instance, why not put an attractive floral arrangement on the island or a large bowl of fruit? Why not put some decorative ornaments near the kitchen window – like a vase with fresh cut flowers from the yard? Some stagers believe in keeping the counters completely bare but I believe this is a mistake. The home should not look that sterile. You'd be amazed at what a tiny bit of enhancement will make in putting a smile on a buyer's face.

Case Study 33

BEFORE

Collections are great but one can surely overdo a collection by trying to display it all at once and in a random, unplanned fashion. This room is so chaotic and mismanaged it would be uncomfortable for most people to stay in the room very long. And if trying to appeal to a buyer, forget it. This room was crying out for some serious professional help.

AFTER

The first thing the professional stager did was remove everything from the wall except for the large painting over the fireplace. What an improvement! Now the real focal point of the room is featured and there are no distracting items on the wall trying to fight for attention. The stager also removed all the papers and items from the coffee table and removed the occasional chair from the room (upper left side). She then brought in a small chest to act as a console behind the left sofa. A plant was placed on the mantel and a small palm in the right corner. This room really turned out lovely and no doubt was very impressive to buyers. Kudos to the stager!

BARB'S COMMENTS: The staging is excellent, but I think just a little more accessorizing would have made it great. A coordinating flower arrangement on the coffee table, with a few hard bound books laid one on the other would have been a nice touch. Some assorted pottery or ceramics in a grouping of 3 on the console/chest would have added some extra charm to the left side of the room. Not much – but just enough to take it to the next level.

Case Study 34

The sconces are placed unusually high on the wall in this narrow bathroom. There is nothing to make one even want to walk in – especially not someone like me who suffers from claustrophobia. Perhaps there had been a mirror on the wall previously – perhaps not. So the question is: How do we make it so the sconces and the sink pedestal look like a united whole?

AFTER
The redesigner brought in a very fancy, decorative mirror that instantly dresses up this bathroom. The towel rod on the right wall has been raised to a higher level to accommodate the decorative towels and tassels and an ornate wall decoration has been placed above the towels. What a charming space this has turned out to be! I love it when a

stager or a redesigner isn't afraid to use items that bring a lot of drama to the space and make it very, very interesting.

BARB'S COMMENTS: The tiny trash basket on the floor to the right of the pedestal is too short for the area and I'd worry about it looking quite unattractive if any refuse is thrown into it. A taller basket with a lid would be preferable. I don't know what that round shaped thing is on the right of the pedestal about 2/3rds the way up. I expect it is part of the plumbing. It would have been nice if this could have been eliminated from view somehow. I do love the tassels on the towels. The mirror appears top heavy for the pedestal but better this than a large gap of space between the sconces and the pedestal.

Case Study 35

BEFORE
The large mirror on the far wall has been inappropriately balanced with a much smaller picture. The curved sofa sectional has been pushed up against the wall of windows. As is often the case, the furniture in the room, including an upright piano, is all placed around the perimeter of the room. So here we have another room in great need of a rearrangement service.

AFTER
Well, unfortunately the redesigner on this project did not make any changes to the placement of the sectional. Too bad. She added some patterned pillows and a poorly placed rectangular area rug. The floor lamp to the left of the sectional is gone, however the piano looks unmoved. I'm afraid this room fails to meet the standards of a professional stager or redesigner.

BARB'S COMMENTS: Pushing this S-shaped sectional up against this corner is just not acceptable. I can't see the whole room, but this just doesn't work, I don't care how many pillows you add nor whether there is an area rug – as a matter of fact, this area rug is also all wrong. If the sectional HAD to go against a wall, it should have been the wall where the mirror hangs. It appears to be the same width as the wall or close to it. As it is, the sectional feels like it is jutting out on its right as it extends past where the windows end. This was a very poor solution to the problem and really didn't address the major issues in the room. Sorry! I included this example as a case study so you'd be able to learn from other people's mistakes as well as their successes or near misses.

Case Study 36

BEFORE
Whew! There's a lot going on in this home office. The good news is there are some interesting and unusual pieces to work with. The bad news is that they are strewn everywhere making the room very hectic, out of control, and probably making it difficult for anyone to get something done at this work station. So let's see how a professional stager worked with the space to improve the situation.

AFTER
The placement of the desk is unchanged. However, gone are all the things clogging up the works. A border of wallpaper has been added. The entire mess on the desk is gone. Yea! A large plant has been placed on the top of the desk unit. This is a much more enticing space. The office chair has been replaced with a simple occasional chair. It is clean and orderly and is a major improvement.

BARB'S COMMENTS: This desk unit just does not fit in this corner. Look at how the left side juts out in front of the blinds on the window. Since I can't see the rest of the room, I can't help but wonder if there wasn't a better alternative as far as placement is concerned. I'm not sure I like the wallpaper border. It does not feel right. It was already there but it would have been better if it had been removed and the wall repainted. The rug looks to be covered with stains. Not sure that leaving it was the right idea, but then those dark patches might also be shadows and not stains or wear problems. I like everything else the stager did here. But the desk clearly needed to be moved to a different location.

Case Study 37

BEFORE
The owner of this home has tried to utilize the central part of
the room, not just the perimeter. But we still have a serious
problem with the arrangements in this room. There are a lot
of undersized pieces which make the room look overly busy
and cluttered. One of the two sofas faces the TV, but the
other one does not. Let's go to work.

AFTER
The professional stager did an excellent job of editing this
room of all the unnecessary furniture and looking for ways to
bring more harmony and balance into the room. She elected
to leave the sofa in front of the window and remove the dark
loveseat. The TV and stand are gone, as well as other tables
that just didn't help the situation. Two unmatched lamps
flank the sofa, as well as two unmatched end tables. I don't
have a major problem with that. Sometimes one needs to

work with what's available and do the best one can. The too small round table has been made to look larger by the white area rug below it. A nice drapery treatment has been added to the window, making a much more dramatic statement while softening the window. Nicely done.

BARB'S COMMENTS: Off hand there is a huge improvement to the room, however, I think I would have pulled the sofa away from the window into the middle of the room and turned it to <u>face</u> the window, making the window the focal point of the room. Looks like there might be a nice view out the window to feature. By pulling the sofa out to face the window, you're still inviting buyers into the room and giving them something to look at in the room the moment they step through the doorway. The two companion pictures on the right wall should be hung side by side, not in a stair-stepped fashion. You only stair-step your pictures over actual steps. The slip cover looks very nice, as do the throw pillows. Had there been another coffee table (preferably rectangular or oblong), it would have been preferable.

Case Study 38

BEFORE
This stager had an empty shell (or house) to work with.
Sometimes vacant rooms are difficult because they are empty
palettes and one can go in a million directions. When there
are an overwhelming number of choices one can make, it
takes a discerning eye to see a vision and dial in on the
vision, blocking out all the other choices that could make
things very confusing. So let's see what the stager created.

AFTER
This is a lovely example of making great choices and not
letting the choices get out of hand. One of the signs of a true
professional is <u>knowing what to do</u>, but also <u>when to stop</u>.
The furnishings chosen for the various sections of the room
are, for the most part, good choices and in good proportion
to the wall, the actual space in the room and in good scale
with each other. Notice that the stager did not try to fill up

the shelves. The furnishings are contemporary to blend with the contemporary features in the room.

BARB'S COMMENTS: The lamp cord should have been more carefully hidden, at least for the picture. I would have tried to place a taller vase on the shelf on the right to fill up more of the vertical space in that area. But this room looks great in the picture so I'm confident it looks even better in reality. Well done, stager.

Case Study 39

This room looks like the movers came and dropped the furniture in the room and left. There is no rhyme or reasoning to the placement of the posters on the wall. They look as if they're floating in space and make the whole room look and feel awkward.

AFTER
The chairs have new slipcovers and probably need them. Four have been evenly spaced around the table. A large framed print has been hung above the buffet, which is far more suitable and in good scale to the buffet. Some accessories and a small tree have also been introduced into the room and it actually looks quite nice.

BARB'S COMMENTS: I like what was done in this room very much. I'm a bit perplexed by the two wine glasses on the table beside the large bowl. I don't know if this picture was taken before the room was completed or if this was a choice of the stager. The slipcovers might have been pressed or de-wrinkled somehow, but that's a minor problem. The tree in the corner should be taller (slightly below the height of the framed print) so it is in better scale with the window. The vase and candle look like soldiers standing at attention on each side. By moving them together into a table vignette and adding a 3rd item, the arrangement on the buffet would be much stronger. The three items should be of different heights and placed approximately 1/3rd of the distance from either the left or the right side of the buffet; odd numbers make the best vignettes.

Case Study 40

BEFORE

A beautiful room with the double floor to ceiling windows, there is a problem with scale and proportions in this room. A simple furniture rearrangement will help immeasurably.

AFTER

Instead of the chair and ottoman out in the middle of the room, the loveseat and a coffee table have been moved to center stage, with the chair as a supporting cast member. The soft window treatment with the tiebacks is a great repetitive example of how repetition can be used to create harmony and unity in a space. The throw pillows and table accessories help to complete this picture in a sensible, attractive manner.

BARB'S COMMENTS: I personally love what the stager or redesigner did in this room. There's probably a fireplace off camera to the right, so it works out perfectly to place the seating facing that direction. I would want to buy this home!

Case Study 41

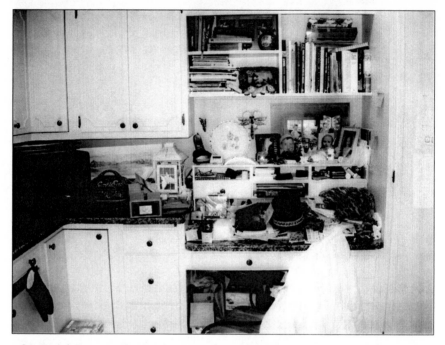

The problem with desk spaces in a kitchen is they often become the catch-all for all sorts of debris. Yes, I said debris. You know how you have something in your hand and you don't know what to do with it then, so you just lay it down somewhere with the intention of coming back later to take care of it? It happens to all of us. This may be a very common sight in many kitchens across the land. It's no way to live and it's certainly no way to sell a home.

AFTER

Have you ever noticed that you tend to keep your bedroom straightened up much better when the bed is made? Well, the same can be said of areas like this. They just seem to attract messes. So the key to avoiding these types of problems is to decide what you're going to do with anything in your hand WHILE it is still in your hand. Break the habit of telling yourself you'll get back to it later. The professional redesigner assigned to this task did a fantastic job of clearing away all of the debris and showcasing this wonderful kitchen feature in this home.

BARB'S COMMENTS: I would have worked harder to balance the wall in the center section. I know it's difficult, particularly since there appears to be an electrical outlet on the left side. But that section needs better balance. I would have removed the decorations hanging down at the top of the tall cabinets on the far right. This looks messy to me, probably because it is so small.

Case Study 42

Clearly this room needs some life at the windows. The cord hanging in the air from the TV to the wall is not pleasing to the eye. The owners do have the sofa out in the middle of the room facing the fireplace. That's good. It shouldn't be too hard to pull this room together.

AFTER
Oops! I was wrong. You can't see it in these black and white pictures, but the redesigner chose to paint all of the walls a bright red – perhaps upon the insistence of the owner. The sofas were either reupholstered or changed out for some off-white sofas. There appears to be a grey and cream colored tile floor with a strong geometric pattern on the floor, with a large gray solid field in the middle. The arrangement of the room looks pretty good. At least the red has been sprinkled around the room. It appears in the artwork over the fireplace and on the throw pillows.

BARB'S COMMENTS: From what I could tell in the color version of this photo, red on the walls was not the best of choices. But some people like massive amounts of color on the walls. If you're going to use color on the walls, it's best to keep it subdued, otherwise the walls dominate everything else in the room. I don't know why the rods for the drapes were placed above the curve of the right window, without any valance or cornice at the top. It does not look good to have the drapery treatment go straight across while the window curves at the top. It's clear the redesigner wanted the window treatments all at the same height for uniformity, but it isn't working out very well in this example. The strong red walls bear no relationship whatsoever to the tile floor nor to the brick fireplace. I think it was a very poor choice. Sorry.

Case Study 43

BEFORE

This large master bedroom looks like it's in the blue funk. It looks and feels dreary. Little attention has been paid to the room. There is no personality. It's just there. So let's see how our redesigner chose to change all that.

AFTER
Well, in the color version the walls were painted a bright peach color. The bed spread has been changed out to a checked yellow, peach and dark pink spread and the window treatment is of the same fabric. A large ottoman has been added to the foot of the bed, and the bed has been given a new head and foot board. A tall chest of drawers has been placed against the wall with a too small painting in the middle of the wall. A smaller coordinating print has been hung above the headboard and more pillows have been added to the bed. In addition the placement of the bed has changed.

BARB'S COMMENTS: I agree with the new placement of the bed. It is better situated in relationship to the entry to the room. There is probably a matching window on the other side of the bed, and if there is, then the bed is centered between the two. It would appear one new nightstand has been added. Don't ever place a chest of drawers immediately back of a door that opens in its direction. This is a good way to mess up the chest as well as the door. And in this case, the chest does not look good all the way off to the far right of the wall. The framed pictured is out of proportion to the wall. It should be substantially larger. The oversized ottoman is a poor choice for the foot of the bed. The depth of the ottoman feels heavy for the bed but it was a nice attempt to provide seating in the room. I would hope the chest could have found a more suitable wall for its size and shape elsewhere in the room. Still it looks better than before.

Case Study 44

BEFORE

A young Jewish couple were trying desperately to figure out how to arrange the furniture in their small living room. The sofa and sofa chair were overly large, overstuffed with different fabrics. They had placed a very nice wooden armoire right in the middle of the wall of windows, which not only blocked the light and view to the front yard, but over time would have harmed the wood of this beautiful piece of furniture. Being devout to their faith, they also wanted to reserve a special place for their daily prayers and reading of the Torah, plus they had a dog cage that needed to stay in the room. The big screen TV in the corner was to soon be placed above the fireplace.

AFTER

The sofa and the sofa chair were rearranged to face each other. The large ottoman was placed between the two to serve as a coffee table. A tray would be used to stabilize any items useful when seated. Since the round glass coffee table was

completely out of scale for such large furniture, it was used as an end table for the loveseat and a smaller matching table was used as the end table for the larger sofa. This

helped to balance the room. A prayer table was placed below the window (upper right) and the room was tidied up. The armoire was moved down the wall to a perfectly sized section to the right of the windows. It all came together nicely.

Case Study 45

BEFORE
Placement of the bed, shelf unit and small desk is crucial in this very tiny bedroom. When the furniture is small, great care needs to be taken to make sure it isn't placed where it can look and feel even smaller. To open up space for a better arrangement in this room, the bed needed to be placed against the opposite wall.

AFTER
By putting the roll top desk and shelf unit near each other, the more utilitarian elements in the room felt better. The bed was pulled away from the long wall so that it is easier to make the bed each morning and to help balance the room.

BARB'S COMMENTS: Try to place like-kind pieces near each other if they are out of proportion to the wall as you see here. This room clearly needed a much larger shelf unit, but none was available. But in this configuration, any person using the desk will find good lighting coming off their left shoulder. The addition of the small print above the desk helped to make that part of the room feel more important and adjusted the scale of the desk to an appropriate height when compared to the height of the window.

Case Study 46

BEFORE
This long living room had a large bay window at the far end.
The owner had two extremely long Asian sofas and only one
long black coffee table, which was only useful to people
sitting on one of the sofas and not the other. The room
wasn't used much, had numerous stains on the white carpet
and was generally unappealing in spite of the nice
furnishings. Since the room was not truly useful, the family
pretty much avoided it and it was really only used at
Christmas when a tree was brought in and decorated. A total
redesign of the room was clearly a must.

AFTER
By repositioning the two matching sofas face to face the
coffee table could easily serve anyone seated on either sofa. A
beautiful TV armoire was moved from a far wall and placed
in front of the window. A console table was placed behind
one sofa against the wall and under the 4 cloisonné plaques

on the wall. To pull the wall grouping closer to the sofa table, an arrangement of 3 geisha dolls was placed on the table. Now upon entering the living room, the eye is drawn straight to the TV cabinet and the great view of their back yard. The room is not only more appealing, it is at the same time much more functional for watching TV or just enjoying family gatherings.

BARB'S COMMENTS: This is a stunning redesign and very cleverly executed. Whenever you have matching sofas (and in particular when they are as long as these) it is difficult to place them in an L-shaped configuration as one might do with a sofa and loveseat. One of the most perfect arrangement techniques available is to place the sofas directly opposite of each other, with a single coffee table between them. It is a useful arrangement, not only because it is so conducive to enjoying intimate conversation with guests, but it is far more functional than any other arrangement might have been. Well done!

Case Study 47

BEFORE

Entries are very important to a home because they help
establish the mood and vibe of the home. Some people enjoy
large entries and others have small ones, as this home had.
What made it even smaller was the staircase to the right just
after one enters (reflected in the mirror). The console
against the wall was a nice piece but too short for the width
of the wall. Entries should be dramatic in some fashion so
the redesigner needed to make the entry provide a stronger
statement for the home.

AFTER

To accomplish a stronger statement in the entry and open up
the space, a large abstract was brought from another room
and hung above the console after the tree was removed.
However, since the abstract was wider and bolder than the
table, the artwork was top heavy. To counter this, two
matching pedestals were place on each side of the table to

add visual weight to the area. While there was only one plant available to put on one the pedestals, the owner would purchase another one for the other side. Some very nice pottery pieces, in the same color palette as the artwork, were placed on the table. The whole look came together quite easily.

BARB'S COMMENTS: This was a nice solution to a bland entry. Many people do not realize how important an entry is. The unfortunate part here is that there is an extremely strong geometric design on the tile floor, which is not exactly pointing to the middle of the table as it should. Sometimes, due to architectural decisions made in advance of a redesigner's help being sought, certain elements cannot be undone. Remember, you can add visual weight on the bottom by extending the width and mass with other pieces.

Case Study 48

BEFORE
This home was really arranged oddly by the couple who live here. Out of sight on the left they had a TV, so they took the sofa and loveseat and pulled them away from the fireplace (at the top center of the photo), completely ignoring the room's main architectural feature. Other furniture floated around in the room made for a hectic, virtually unusable room so no wonder the client called out to a redesigner for help.

AFTER
The redesigner moved the TV from the left wall in the above picture to the right wall over near the TV. By putting the TV near the fireplace, the redesigner could then reposition the sofa and loveseat facing both the fireplace and the TV at the same time. Some temporary arrangements were place in front of the fireplace and on the mantel, and the homeowner

was going to purchase something else more suitable. The owner was also going to purchase a larger TV stand and use the current one elsewhere later. Whenever possible it is good to put a TV close to a fireplace as was done here. The excess loveseat and chaise were moved to other rooms in the home.

BARB'S COMMENTS: The mirror over the fireplace was initially hung too high, leaving a gap of wall between the mantel and the base of the mirror. Since it was not possible to move the mirror down without leaving damage to the wall, the accessories chosen for the mantel needed to be much taller than shown in the first picture. This was changed later by the homeowner. An area rug under the coffee table would help unite the seating arrangement with the rest of the space and act as a nice bridge for all the colors in the room.

Case Study 49

BEFORE
The homeowner's guest bedroom had been neglected. The furniture was sporadically arranged in the room, with the chest of drawers and desk placed where they felt too small for the wall and, therefore, out of proportion. The accessories on the chest of drawers were also out of scale and the room appeared messy and visually unappealing. Call in the redesigner to address these easy-to-fix problems.

AFTER
The redesigner moved the chest of drawers over by the desk to more adequately fill the wall at the foot of the bed. This freed up the wall for some well chosen artwork. The grouping of 3 images nicely fills the wall and makes a bold statement. By combining the two chests of drawers and desk together, it gives the appearance of built-ins and together they create a furniture grouping in good proportion to the wall.

Case Study 50

BEFORE

Can you imagine trying to work in a bedroom turned home office? Stuff everywhere! Clutter galore! How can a person think? If your rooms are de-cluttered and organized you'd really be amazed at how much clearer your mind becomes. One of the big no-no's here is a loveseat pushed up against the window. The loveseat is wider than the window and just looks funny where it is. A redesigner comes to the rescue, thankfully.

AFTER

By repositioning the loveseat against the left wall, the redesigner was able to hang one of the client's favorite prints on the wall above the loveseat. No longer does the loveseat block view of the window and it is easier to open and shut the blinds as well. The room instantly looks and feels better from the moment you enter and it looks far less cluttered.

BARB'S COMMENTS: Now the homeowner can enjoy watching the TV while seated at the desk, but he can watch it from the loveseat as well. Some editing of messy papers and other fixtures in the room helped restore order and attractiveness to this room. Well done.

Case Study 51

BEFORE
While the dark paneling is pretty, it also looks a bit dated.
When selling a home you want the home to look light and
airy and as spacious as possible. Dark walls, even paneled
walls, can be foreboding. The beautiful roll top desk and
dining chairs melt into the scene leaving no contrast to set
them off. The stager went to work to make some dramatic
changes.

AFTER
The paneling was painted one color on top and painted white
on the bottom with dark chair rail added. Now the desk and
the chairs pop out and you can see the fine design lines. An
elaborate grouping was created using shelves, artwork,
plants, candles, clock and other elements. A large oval area

rug was added under the dining room table. Very nicely done.

BARB'S COMMENTS: This might be a little too much treatment for a staging project. It's difficult to say given the style of the home and the furnishings. The proof would lie in whether the home sold quickly or not. As a redesign project, however, the room looks full, well covered and very attractive. The elaborate wall grouping is well placed and beautifully done. It does appear a bit top heavy, however, but I still like the results. The chairs flanking the roll top desk could be exchanged for visually heavier chairs and that would correct the top heavy feeling on this wall.

Case Study 52

Talk about sterile and lacking any warmth or interest – this bath needs some accessories to dress it up and even cause a buyer to want to use it. Right now it's pretty cold and the window treatment is very odd – and the window frame is much too dark. Strange.

AFTER
With a little creativity and imagination, and a few choice accessories along with a new window treatment, you can feel the luxury increase. The stager turned this cold, cold, cold bath into a spa-like setting, filled with warmth, romance and

excitement. Don't be afraid to include framed artwork in a bathroom. With good ventilation, it will not be harmed by steam or water. Soften those hard edges of a too dark window frame with soft sheers. This room was just crying out for a romantic touch and that's just what the stager gave it.

BARB'S COMMENTS: I love to see students grab hold of their training and utilize every bit of it in their designs. It would have been nice to see the dark color on the window frames turned to white or another pastel, but I'm supposing it was impossible to do it. At any rate, by bringing in some other dark accessories, it helps to settle down the huge impact the window frames have in the room. So it brings up a good point: Whenever you have an odd color that pops out and draws attention to a lesser part of the room, add more of that color into the room to help make the offending element less dominant if you can't get rid of the color altogether.

Case Study 53

BEFORE
There are some major mistakes in the furniture arrangement of this room. We have a sofa and matching loveseat placed on opposite sides of the room. There are two green chairs at the far end of the room blocking view of multiple

mismatched furniture pieces. The very dated large lamp on the table towers over the sofa. There are nice pieces in the room, but they are utilized in a very poor manner.

AFTER
A redesigner was called in to help out. After the room was repainted and a wallpaper border added to the top of the walls to simulate crown molding, the room got a major rearrangement. The console/cabinet at the far end was centered under the mirror. The tree was moved to the other corner and the Asian room divider was removed. While the sofa remained where it was, the loveseat was moved to the

far end and angled. An interesting carousel pony was brought in for further interest and a large area rug placed in front of the sofa. The area rug helps to anchor the seating arrangement and blends the two coffee tables into the design so they don't stick out so much.

Beautiful throw pillows now tie the whole color scheme into the room and place color on the light sofa and loveseat. A new, expanded wall grouping has been placed over the sofa, along with two wall-mounted candle holders. The matching green chairs have been brought to the foreground, helping to balance the colors in the room for a much more pleasing effect. The tall lamp is gone, thank goodness.

BARB'S COMMENTS: Not sure I would have elected to put the loveseat at an angle. But it's difficult to tell whether there was room to manage it another way. I think the redesigner did an amazing job in pulling this room together and balancing out the colors in the room. A job well done and kudos to the redesigner.

Case Study 54

BEFORE
It's always a visual problem whenever the furniture exceeds
the width of the wall as seen here. It is important to try to
avoid this look at all costs. The situation is made even worse

because the sofa is darker than the walls and the windows.
To make matters worse, there is no art or wall treatments
between the two windows, so one's attention is drawn most
specifically to the completely blank wall.

AFTER
Beautiful window treatments closer to the color of the sofa
have been added. A large framed reproduction and a
decorative half moon carved wall ornament dress up that
blank, boring wall. While the redesigner decided to keep the
sofa where it was, the darker window treatments help make
the width of the sofa feel more appropriate from a
proportional point of view. By placing the two end tables

closer to the sofa, they also help make the grouping feel more size appropriate as they extend from the outer side of one window to the outer side of the opposite window, and the lamps appear centered in front of the windows.

BARB'S COMMENTS: At first glance, one would be impressed with the improvement the redesigner was able to achieve, particularly with the window and wall treatments. However, I remain troubled by the furniture placement. There appears to be two matching recliners, one on one end of the room, and one on the other end. This makes for an overly long placement of furniture that feels odd to me. The tray on the ottoman doubling as a coffee table looks precarious and somewhat dangerous to me and it is not the best scale for the sofa either. I love the feeling that was created in this room, but I think the furniture arrangement is weak and there no doubt were better options available. To minimize an overly long room, try to place the sofa at a right angle to the longest wall to make the room appear wider.

Case Study 55

BEFORE
Where there is no art on the walls, a room surely looks
unfinished, as if someone were just moving in or about to
move out. Accessories are some of the most important pieces
to be placed in a room because they carry the personality.
While we tend to de-personalize rooms when staging a home
for sale, it does not include removing the artwork – but it
does include removing family photographs, religious
artifacts and so forth. So let's see what the redesigner did
with this room.

AFTER

The two companions with the sconces is nicely proportioned to the wall space. That's the good part. Unfortunately the redesign falls apart after that. For one thing, the bench and small table are under-scaled for the wall and the artwork. It therefore makes the art grouping feel overbearing and pressing down on the furniture; worse, there is a significant gap between the base of the art and the top of the bench. The fairly tall plant on the pedestal built into the wall is too tall, cutting off part of the wall. When that happens the grouping no longer looks centered on the wall.

BARB'S COMMENTS: This wall would look better if the furniture was not placed against the wall. A visually heavy buffet or long chest or bookcase would have been a better choice. If none were available, it would have been better to lower the art arrangement and leave the rest of the wall bare, as it is a walk-by wall anyway. The bold, dramatic mats on the art are dark and very strong – too strong for the art and too strong for the airy, ornate bench and table below.

Case Study 56

BEFORE
If you always make your bed everyday as soon as you get up,

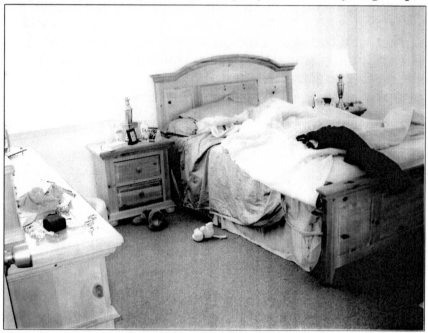

the whole room will look and feel much better and act as an incentive to keep the room less cluttered and messy. It's a proven fact. This home, however, wants to go on the market for a quick sale, so some drastic improvements are necessary.

AFTER
Well, we definitely have an improvement here, though there are some problems as well. First off, the bed has been made and a quilted comforter added with matching pillows, along with some additional throw pillows. Two matching lamps have been kept, but the mess has been removed, and that, in itself, improves the situation. However there are arrangement issues that need to be addressed as the placement of the bed and end tables was not changed in any

way. The white window treatments are generally fine for staging a room, but in this case do nothing to help balance the room.

BARB'S COMMENTS: Where to begin. As stated earlier, the bed's position is poor. If the far right night stand had been removed, the bed and left night stand could have been shifted to the right so that the bed would be situated dead center on the wall. This would have prevented the left night stand from sitting half way in front of the window (not good). Just because the furniture is there, that doesn't mean it should all stay in the room. The off centered problem is accentuated by the too dark artwork arrangement over the bed. The art grouping is too strong; it's jarring and draws too much attention to itself. The small print on the far right wall is much too small and out of proportion. Small prints like this should only be used in large groupings or on very narrow wall panels. It is also hung way too high. While this design is an improvement, it still has many issues.

Case Study 57

BEFORE

I have a feeling there is a TV or fireplace off to the left in this room, which would explain why the sofa is placed where it is. The main problem is one of clutter – lots of clutter. There are stuffed animals, blankets, memorabilia, papers and plants in unusual places – all too much going on here. So a major cleanup was in order.

AFTER

It's amazing what good organization skills can do for a room, even if most of the major pieces and accessories remain in the same spot. Many people unfortunately believe that buyers can look past the mess and still want to buy the home. But this is clearly not the case. I'm not clear on whether this is a redesigned room for a homeowner staying in the home or whether it will go on the market for sale, but clearly the room looks so much better now. Over the years people often get caught up in bringing in more and more stuff and get a bit lazy once the room seems beyond help.

BARB'S COMMENTS: The grouping on the wall has been hung too close to the window. Even though there is a high backed chair in the corner; it just doesn't look well placed, particularly from this angle. Before locking in a wall arrangement (particularly one so close to the edge of the wall) make sure it is well framed by the wall on <u>all</u> sides. This arrangement feels awkward precisely because it was placed too far to the right. This one adjustment would have made that corner look far better. I'm a little uncomfortable with the sofa cutting this large window in half. I would be interested in seeing the rest of the room to know if it was a good idea or not. If there is a TV or fireplace on the left wall (out of sight), then the placement of the sofa makes sense.

Case Study 58

BEFORE
Normally one would look at a picture this size and feel it was scaled appropriately for the bed and the wall between the two posts. But for some reason things just don't feel right. In this example it may surprise you to learn that sometimes breaking the rules is more effective than holding to them.

Bedroom 1 Before

AFTER
The redesigner hired to work on this room brought in the matching end table for the right side of the bed. Two matching lamps help set off the bed nicely and balance the wall. The tree sculpture on the wall would normally be considered poor scale in relationship to the bed and poor proportions for the wall, but somehow I like this better than the framed print in the before picture.

Bedroom1 After

BARB'S COMMENTS: Sometimes the most effective designs are the ones that break the rules. By going more austere and simple with an Asian feeling (removing the strong plaid blanket at the foot of the bed), and adding to the throw pillows at the head of the bed, this example looks quite lovely and it works for me. The tree ornament on the wall could have been raised up, however, as it appears ready to fall down behind the pillows. Always turn the lamp shades so that the seam is against the wall, not out in front as you see on the right lamp. For the sake of the after picture, the comforter should have been tucked into the frame on the right side of the bed as it is on the left side.

I know, I know – I'm picky. But that's how you'll learn and remember, right?

Case Study 59

BEFORE
I wrote earlier about putting artwork in a bathroom. Clearly this homeowner had no problem putting art in the bathroom, but the question is: Is the art too strong or too large for the space? I know you can't see this in color, but the image over the toilet is dominant blue while the image facing the sink (on far right) is red and green and white.

PowderRoom1 Before

So to start with, we have a serious balance issue created by the strong changes in color palette in the art and because of the size of the art, therefore, the bathroom looks overly narrow.

AFTER
The first thing the redesigner/stager did in this bathroom was to repaint the top part of the walls with a softer color. In this case she chose a medium gold tone, leaving the

beadboard white. Then she replaced the artwork with smaller images more suitable to the size of the room. She also placed a large plant on the top of the toilet tank which helps draw the toilet and the art print together, thus making the elements against that wall look and feel more united. The colors in the two art prints hung side by side on the far right blend nicely with the color scheme and the entire bathroom is far more pleasant and inviting. It no longer feels overdone.

PowderRoom1 After

BARB'S COMMENTS: This is a wonderful example of how important art is in a room. Not only does it need to be the right size and shape, but the colors need to blend in the room. Notice how the print over the toilet does not exceed the width of the toilet as in the before picture. By always making sure the pieces or elements on the bottom are wider than on top, you can usually avoid accidentally creating a top heavy feeling. Excellent job! Can you see how much wider the bathroom looks now?

Case Study 60

BEFORE

This homeowner has a very large white or off white entertainment center appropriately placed in the middle of the wall. She has two matching artificial trees on each end to complete the wall which, if you saw it in color, you would know to be an orange wall. On the left wall is a sofa and on the right appears to be a chaise. I'm actually quite impressed with the arrangements on the shelves, in particular the opening in the middle.

AFTER

Now let's take a look at what the redesigner on this project did. Oh boy. I'm happy to see some of the greenery on top of the unit was removed. The redesigner added some extra height by arranging the clock, urn and another object on the top center section. But I feel the client's own arrangement in the section just above the TV is superior to the one the redesigner created, which is unfortunate. I also feel the shelves are much more crowded and too busy, though she did a good job of filling the vertical height as well as the horizontal width of the shelves. However one side is much darker than the other. Her table arrangement looks better than before.

BARB'S COMMENTS: The two metal ornaments high on the wall above the trees should be removed or else moved in closer to the center accessories to form one complete grouping over the entertainment center. That whole end of the room appears very complicated and really is not as sharp as it could be. I think the redesigner tried to incorporate too much in the unit, especially for such a contemporary unit, which lends so much better to a simplified arrangement. But perhaps she was asked to do so by the client. The ultra strong white entertainment center really stands out too much, for me, and this hurts the overall design of the room in my humble opinion. But as redesigners, we must work with what the client has in the home, so there are limitations to what one can do.

Case Study 61

BEFORE
When selling a home it's important to remember that potential buyers will open up your pantry and look inside. Now you can either empty it out or look for ways to make it look organized and neat. As part of the staging of this home, the professional tackled this tedious job and let's take a look at how she fared.

AFTER

One way to instantly organize a pantry is to place items of like kinds or sizes together. Notice the cereal containers on the third shelf from the top. Place all canned goods together. Turn all labels to face the front. Edit where possible. Place larger items toward the bottom or on the lower shelves. In this case, I feel more editing should have been done if this home was to go on the market.

BARB'S COMMENTS: When staging, less is definitely more. This pantry is still too full. Put all taller items on the lower shelves to give visual support.

Case Study 62

BEFORE
This room has an interesting architectural feature in that the window walls are angled to the wall with the door. Yet the owner of this home did not pay any attention to the angle of the walls when placing the table in the space. The little items sitting on the window sills make the room feel cluttered. They are way too small to have any impact and just look messy.

AFTER
The stager corrected the angle of the table and removed the items from the window sills. The chairs were rearranged neatly and two of the four chairs have nice place settings. A more appropriate centerpiece was also added to replace the

previous plant. Simple changes, yes. But, oh, so necessary and effective they are.

BARB'S COMMENTS: Pay attention to angles. They are very important in determining the correct furniture placement. Placement can make or break a room and it can certainly have a detrimental effect on selling a home if it is not correctly done. One element that stagers worry about is the inclusion of tableware (knives, forks and spoons). It would probably be very, very rare for this to cause a problem, but when you consider that many buyers bring their children with them, and children are curious little beings, it's better to be safe than sorry. You can still make a nice table setting without the silverware.

Case Study 63

BEFORE
Just like the pantry in an earlier case study, the closets in the home are also places that potential buyers will open and inspect. It's not so much that they're snoops, but they want to check out the condition, the depth and the spaciousness. Most people have a lot of clothes, so the more storage they perceive a home has, the better they like it. If a closet is full of stuff and it's messy inside, it's a huge detriment to selling the home.

AFTER

Here the stager took out all of the purses and other items from off the shelf and left it completely bare. She left a few organized coats and jackets and it appears there is a hamper on the far right. The poster has been removed as well as any extra hangers. There is enough left in the closet to show how ample the storage capacity is, yet not so much as to make it too full.

BARB'S COMMENTS: A packed closet sends the message, "There isn't enough storage space in this house." So leave a few garments but make all the closets look especially spacious.

Case Study 64

BEFORE
It's obvious from this view that the sofa sectional, coffee table and end tables are positioned too far away from the room's main focal point, the fireplace. If the seating is too far away, it creates <u>screaming distance</u> and removes any feeling of intimacy and unity in the room. It's amazing what just a few feet of space differential can make.

AFTER
To illustrate what I mean, notice that a console (sofa table) has been placed at the back of the sofa, which has been moved forward and closer to the fireplace. Just this one addition and change has made all the difference in the world to this room. By adding the console back of the sofa, it serves to break up the bland visual <u>wall</u> that the back of the sofa creates. The stager can now place some nice accessories on the console to add more interest to this part of the room.

BARB'S COMMENTS: In reality when designing a room for living, one would seek to retain a way to have lighting in the room. However, when staging a room, one can eliminate the end tables and the lamps. A bit sneaky, I admit, but a way to show a more intimate room arrangement. The goblet on the lower right shelf is too short for the shelf space. From what I can see in this shot, the room looks fabulous.

Case Study 65

BEFORE
The owner painted the top part of the wall red above the soffit but the left wall looks to be painted gold to repeat the color of the cabinetry. The refrigerator is white while all the other appliances are black. All of these colors really break up the look of this kitchen, making it look more busy than normal. To add insult to injury, there are a zillion photos on the refrigerator, the counters are covered with lots of stuff, the island is a mess and it all looks quite hectic.

AFTER
The stager removed all the chaos by clearing away the island and counter tops. All of the photos and magnets are gone from the refrigerator, thank goodness. It would have been

nice if an electrical plate the color of the cabinetry had been used instead of leaving the white one (on the island) as it is so center stage in this photo.

BARB'S COMMENTS: Notice that the stager left most of the plants and accessories on the top shelf above the upper cabinets. I would have liked to see more attention paid to the spacing of the plants. Perhaps it's just the angle that tricks the eye into believing the right shelf area is much fuller than the left one. I think the stager left a large plant in the middle of each shelf, but also placed some accessories in the corner between the two. When you're taking your after pictures, try to watch out for things of this nature that can throw off your finished look simply because of the reference point of the camera. Make adjustments as necessary just for the photo; then readjust afterwards. This way you'll always have after photos that look as great as possible. Not sure I would have kept the red walls myself – too risky for most buyers.

Case Study 66

BEFORE
This owner placed a very tall china cabinet (hutch) nearly in the middle of the far wall. I expect the reason it is slightly offset to the right is because of the door in the upper left corner. So we have this huge piece dominating the wall but out of proportion to the wall if left on its own. Next we have the rectangular table with six chairs placed with the longest side perpendicular to the cabinet, which makes the room look longer as a result.

AFTER
The redesigner wisely looked for ways to correct the proportional problem of the cabinet against the wall by hanging some wall decoration above the two small tables (which are totally dwarfed by the cabinet). Then the

redesigner changed the direction of the table. You can see how much better this looks and how the horizontal line of the table makes the room and the china cabinet appear wider. The elongated table runner repeats the horizontal line

as do the two chairs placed side by side on each side of the table. This is a much more effective placement for the table.

BARB'S COMMENTS: The two tables flanking this massive cabinet are just too small, too overwhelmed by the size differential to feel good. Even with the wall decorations (which help), it just doesn't work. You've really got to be careful to choose pieces in better scale to the other pieces otherwise it makes the cabinet look even bigger and more massive than it really is. A better solution would have been to offset the cabinet to one side or the other and add in a narrow but tall tree on one side to help fill the wall and add enough visual bulk to match up to the size of the china cabinet. Congratulations to the redesigner for making the room more attractive anyway. It does look better but still has problems.

Case Study 67

BEFORE
Sorry to say, you can tell this is a man's office. No offense,
but men often hang wall décor in random places and too
high to make sense. See how unbalanced the back wall has
become. We've got two diplomas trying to balance off with a
file cabinet with shelf unit and two shadow boxes. The desk
is covered with random papers and there is quite a lot of
clutter everywhere.

AFTER
The redesigner left the desk in the same spot but did remove
the tiny, thin chair rail from every wall. The file cabinet and
shelf unit were pushed to the corner and a matching one
brought in and set side by side, increasing the overall size to
a more suitable one from a proportional standpoint. This was
a good move.

BARB'S COMMENTS: Unless there is a solid wood cabinet underneath the two diplomas (far right corner), you cannot expect to balance a heavy shelf unit with two small diplomas on the right. This is a problem with an otherwise good attempt. In addition, the two shadow boxes on the left wall with the picture in the middle are hung too far apart. They are hung to <u>fill up</u> the space instead of forming a real grouping and so one becomes aware of the fact the designer is trying to force them to fill up the wall. This is a mistake.

Don't ever put a trash basket out against a wall in plain sight of visitors. Find a more hidden area in the room, even under the desk. The small plant stand with plant is totally out of scale for the tall shelf unit to the left of it. The stand should have been removed from the room and the plant placed on one of the shelves. This was a great attempt to fix this office's many problems. In large part it succeeded, but there remain some pesky problems I noted above.

Case Study 68

BEFORE
Here is another example of a sofa pushed against a window that is smaller than the width of the sofa. This just makes the sofa appear to be forced into the arrangement. The size of the

sofa is also crowding the space of the two end tables. Two small corner shelves have been attached to the wall high up on both corners. While the arrangement helps to pull one into the room, it really doesn't work for scale and proportional reasons.

AFTER
The redesigner or stager pulled the sofa away from the window and out into the middle of the room facing the window. Excellent choice. The two wing backed chairs are then placed at an angle, one in each corner. A nice console table in brought in to bring drama to the window area and break up all that white. The two lamps are rearranged, with

one on an end table and the other one on the console. More wall ornaments are put up, but the corner shelves remain in place. The other end table winds up in the foreground with a large plant placed on top.

BARB'S COMMENTS: I'm guessing that I would have saved the console to put behind the sofa. Any time you have a sofa out in the middle of the room, you're going to create a huge barrier in the room and it's so helpful to have a nicely decorated console to put behind the sofa to break up that barrier with something decorative. I would have put one of the end tables in the middle of the window and moved the chairs further into the room on each side rather than all the way into the corners. I would have removed the two corner shelves and found another place for them. If I didn't have a place for the other end table and lamp, I would have put the lamp on the console behind the sofa and put the other table in another room. Be willing to experiment with ideas and don't get too locked into those walls and corners. The arrangement on the console needs strengthening as well.

Case Study 69

BEFORE
Do you ever find your dining room table evolving into little more than a utilitarian surface – good for providing a

convenient spot for just about anything and everything? One of the ways to keep this from happening is to make sure you have it adequately decorated. Somehow a huge floral arrangement or a beautiful centerpiece would help keep the table clear and free of all the odds and ends of daily living.

AFTER
There is no better time to keep that table looking beautiful than when you're trying to sell your home. Stagers know the power of beautiful table arrangements. Having a beautifully decorated dining room table sublimely tells prospective buyers that someone enjoys living and eating in the home. It really helps buyers see themselves and their family gathered

around the breakfast table – or helps them envision throwing a party or sharing an intimate dinner with good friends or family members. It reminds them of the importance of family time. This professional stager really created a warm, intimate feeling. One can almost see good friends gathered around for breakfast with a cup of hot chocolate, delicious sweet rolls and steaming hot scrambled eggs.

BARB'S COMMENTS: Note how the casual stools work so

well with the casual dishes. There's no pretense here. The bowl of fruit in the middle of the table adds color and flavor to the whole atmosphere. It is a simple arrangement yet oh so inviting and relaxing. Great job!

Case Study 70

BEFORE
Haven't we all been here at some time in our life? In an attempt to create a cozy, casual kitchen, we sometimes get

carried away with knick knacks everywhere, baskets hung here and there, lots of little plaques and sayings and special mementos from our vacations, the children's little school projects, country towels and so forth. They provide great memories for you and the family but not that impressive to potential buyers.

AFTER
To present a kitchen in a house for sale, one must really strip down all the unnecessary clutter and clean the whole kitchen from top to bottom. Clearly this is what the professional stager did here, but with a few exceptions. All of the wall decorations are gone and most of the items from the counters have been removed as well. The kitchen opens up

and looks much more spacious and there are few distractions for potential buyers to cope with.

BARB'S COMMENTS: The stager didn't go far enough. The towel on the oven should have disappeared, as well as the small area rug in front of the sink (both are pink and blue). The utilitarian box in foreground (teal) on left counter is not decorative enough and none of these items coordinate with the orange flowers on right counter near refrigerator (I know you can't see the color, but I can). But at least the kitchen looks to be clean and clutter free. While it is an improvement, it's not the best staging I've ever seen to be sure.

Case Study 71

BEFORE
I love wall groupings but this one is simply out of control.
The focal point in the room is completely overtaken by the

ornamentation on the wall. The furniture arrangement is
completely dysfunctional, both in regards to the TV and to
the fireplace. Chaos reigns! The talents of a good redesigner
are clearly needed here – this room is nothing short of a
disaster.

AFTER
The first important improvement the redesigner made was
the removal of all of the pictures and various arts and crafts
items scattered all over the wall. The tall black curio cabinet
has been moved elsewhere. The TV has been moved to the
opposite corner (a very good move) where it remains close to
the fireplace. This allows the sofa to be placed so that
someone can enjoy a warm crackling fire at the same time

they are enjoying a good movie on the television. This is the ideal situation. A single large print has been hung over the mantel where just a few tasteful accessories have also been arranged. Since the angle of the TV creates an automatic void behind the TV, a reasonably tall tree has been placed behind it – I would assume the tree is artificial. Many of the other accessories sitting on the floor have been removed. The sofa and the two sofa chairs have been arranged closer to accommodate conversation while maintaining full enjoyment and use of the room.

BARB'S COMMENTS: The room has recovered from the disaster quite nicely. I think the mantel is still a bit too cluttered and there appears to be more questionable accessories and plants on the ledge along the front of the window, but overall we see a major improvement in how the room looks and how it functions for the homeowner. Some darker throw pillows on the two light pink chairs would help distribute the dark colors in the room for better balance.

Case Study 72

BEFORE
It is very common for people to hang shelves and wall
decorations much too high over beds – well, over most

things for that matter. I just don't know why they insist on
creating these huge gaps of space between what's on the wall
and what's underneath. Clearly this bedroom needs the
expert touches of a professional redesigner to solve its
problems.

AFTER
The redesigner wisely moved the bed from its present
location under the shelf to the other wall. Making the bed
always looks better too. In this case more throw pillows have
been added, along with a folded quilt at the foot of the bed.
These additions help the bed look wider and more spacious.
Many of the pictures placed on the shelves have been

redesigned and coordinated into an impressive wall grouping above the bed, hung close enough to the pillows to be seen as a total grouping or united whole. Well done! The larger pictures have been arranged on the bottom of the grouping to give it visual weight on the bottom and smaller items have been hung above. Very nicely done. A chest of drawers has been moved below the shelf which appears not to have been moved at all. By placing a decorative box on top of the chest to close the gap, the redesigner found the perfect solution for this wall as well. Additional accessories have been added to the shelf and the whole room comes together beautifully.

BARB'S COMMENTS: This is an excellent example of redesign at its best. The redesigner took what the client already owned, and by simply rearranging the entire room, she took this formerly unloved, messy, badly arranged room and turned it into a charming, relaxing guest room or place to escape for a good read or a nap. Very well done. Kudos to the redesigner.

Case Study 73

BEFORE
The key to a functional, workable home office is

organization. This isn't just a home office for one person –
two people work here and they each have the same tolerance
for messes it would seem. But this has to be eliminated if this
house is to be sold. Even if it isn't going on the market, this
room needs major help.

AFTER
To help encourage these two clutter bugs from returning to
old habits, the stager placed a beautiful bouquet of white
flowers on the counter between the two stations. This is a
subtle way of reminding everyone to keep the work stations
neat and orderly. All of the loose papers have been gathered
up and stored out of sight or thrown away. The messy trash
bins have been removed or stored out of sight. The shelves

have been de-cluttered some but looks like more could have been done. Yes, one must have the ability to work effectively but a clutter free office is much more conducive to productivity. A few decorative accessories have been positioned here and there to encourage cleanliness and a sense of design and order.

BARB'S COMMENTS: Built in book shelves are very handy to have. The problem is that unless the homeowner is meticulously organized, they can easily become storage spots for all sorts of messiness. I much prefer more cabinets with doors to hide the items that don't contribute to the decorative look of the space, but that's just me. But by interspersing some decorative accessories in with the books and manuals, the home office can still look much like a home and less like an office.

Case Study 74

Just love that empty room after it has been freshly painted.

It's such an open palette with a myriad of possibilities, all equally wonderful. A home stager must come up with good ideas to romance the room, help buyers fall in love with the room and whet their appetite as to the room's full potential.

AFTER
This stager brought in a beautiful sleigh bed to fill the room and demonstrate how spacious it is. A small antique desk was placed on the narrow wall panel between the two windows. A vertically formatted work of art is hung above the desk with a few accessories overlapping at the base. Notice how asymmetric the windows are: a large double pane window on the far right of the room, and a short sliver on the left. Extra wide white panel drapes are placed on both

sides of the room ignoring the width of the window on the left. The tiebacks for the window treatments are unique making the room quite unique and interesting. Two beautiful floor plants create a tropical ambience that compliments the throw pillows on the bed. There is a lot of natural light in the

room, but care was taken to provide a bedside lamp for the evening hours.

BARB'S COMMENTS: I love to see creative people at work. The professional redesigner/stager who designed this room is both practical and romantic. The roll top desk will appear in better proportion to the wall when the drapes are closed and it would have been better, perhaps, to shoot the room with the drapes closed. But I think this room looks lovely. I'm a bit puzzled by the shape and placement of the area rug which you can see in the lower right corner of the picture. This is a question mark for me because the bed appears to sit half on the rug and half off the rug, but otherwise the room is an outstanding success.

Case Study 75

BEFORE
Here is another example of a stone cold empty room. There is a sun room out towards the right side and the room sports very tall walls. I'm not 100% sure this is a home but for the sake of the Case Study we'll say it is. A stager has been hired to make the space look beautiful and let's see what she did to solve the inherent problems.

AFTER
A large contemporary shelf unit has been backed up to the only large wall in the space. A few selected accessories have been placed here and there. A large teal sofa combined with a matching chair and ottoman sit in an L-shaped configuration in the middle of the room facing the large windows. Two matching barrel chairs with a round table complete the

arrangement on the other side. Normally this would be ok but there are problems.

BARB'S COMMENTS: The two open armed club chairs are much too small and light in visual weight to be matched with this overstuffed sofa, chair and ottoman. It would really be better if they weren't there. Sometimes by bringing in furniture that is the wrong scale you wind up emphasizing the disparity rather than solving your problem. The stager should have just let the sofa combination carry the room. No attempt was made to try to make the chairs look heavier. This is just a really poor choice of furniture combinations.

Case Study 76

BEFORE
BEFORE
We all love to dress up the mantel on our fireplace but this
stream of pictures, all relatively the same size with a clock
between just isn't getting the job done right. It appears there

are a couple of dog beds in front of the hearth. The furniture
looks to be arranged quite well but it is the accessorizing that
is the major issue here. A redesigner is brought in to address
these issues.

AFTER
Obviously the dog beds had to go elsewhere. One just can't
ruin the room's natural focal point with dog beds, can one?
Next the redesigner removed all the items from the mantel
leaving it bare. Actually it really isn't a mantel – it's just a
row of bricks on top which could serve as a mantel if needed.
Two nicely arranged companions framed exactly alike are

hung on the wall. It is appropriate that they be side by side and hung close to each other and close to the brick. The proportions for the wall are perfect in this case. The fireplace provides the perfect amount of visual weight below to support them. On either side, the redesigner hung two more prints, lower than the others. It's difficult to say whether this was the best idea or not as they tend to detract from the two over the fireplace and the wall is in danger of being overdone with art. But it is what it is at this point.

BARB'S COMMENTS: The visual appeal of this room works much better than before. It would have been very nice if the redesigner had planned a way for the small white speakers of the surround system to be less noticeable (the right one doesn't show in this picture, but it's there). The accessories on the coffee table look much better than before.

Case Study 77

BEFORE
Random furniture arrangements never work out very well.

This home clearly has a random color palette as well as being oddly arranged. There is no focal point and the eye is left to seek out some place to rest. There is no direction given in the design and layout of the room. It is a room crying out for help.

AFTER
The professional re-arranger started by repositioning the sofa. When you get the sofa in the right place, everything else somehow seems to work out. The green chair has been paired with the sofa to form an L-shaped arrangement, working with the angles. An area rug has been introduced to help anchor the seating arrangement. On the rear wall a sofa table (console) is effectively used as a visual support to the

lamp, plant and artwork. A floor plant anchors the corner to visually support another framed print hung on the narrow panel of wall just to the right of the window. I don't see a coffee table, but clearly the odd green table formerly used for this purpose has been removed, thank goodness. The re-arranger of this room has created a very nice arrangement for the room and I would bet there is a fireplace or TV on the other side of the room out of sight.

BARB'S COMMENTS: I dislike skinny sconces as they are usually in very poor scale no matter where or how they are used by most people, so I'm happy to see they were removed. Notice how the portrait on the narrow wall on the far left is facing the window. This is what you want. You want any left/right directional artwork to point the attention into the room, not out of the room. This room has clearly received a major improvement. It is restful to the eye. It is organized and completely makes sense. A job well done by the professional hired to correct the problems in the room.

Case Study 78

BEFORE
The walls in this room are painted a fairly strong green.
Many of the accessories are also green, as are the plants. The

homeowner obviously has children and you can see the
impact children leave on a home. But since the owner
wanted to make the room more pleasing to the eye and more
functional, the services of a professional redesigner were
acquired.

AFTER
While many of the unusual wall décor was retained, it was
adjusted by the redesigner into a more pleasing
arrangement. The white painted brick was repainted a light
tan, to pick up the tan in the plaid sofa. The walls were
repainted a subdued yellow though I don't know why. An
area rug, the same color as the repainted brick, was

introduced. The seating arrangement is the very common L-shaped configuration. A desk area in the back (upper left) has been tidied up but there still seems to be an awfully lot going on in this room.

BARB'S COMMENTS: The rearrangement of the seating is a definite plus. I'm also in favor of the cosmetic changes to the walls and fireplace. I'm finding it very difficult, however, to appreciate the grouping above the mantel. The skinny lamp on the far left is troublesome. I can't marry the type of wall décor with the rest of the room. The coffee table still seems very untidy and cluttered. Yes, there is a significant improvement in this room, but it still falls flat for the most part. As I wrote earlier, I don't see the connection of the yellow walls with the rest of the décor, which appears to be quite blue. I remain troubled by this room.

Case Study 79

BEFORE
So let's talk about shelf units. This unit appears to be a built-in unit. The bottom six shelves are painted white, but the

background to the upper shelf (which is double side) is a darker tan or custard color. As you can see, it is completely bare except for one framed picture. Let's see what our stager did with this blank slate.

AFTER
The professional stager chose to place a set of 3 grouped accessories on each of the lower shelves. The distribution of color isn't quite the best. Many of the items appear to be very similar in height. In some places the items are so small they leave huge gaps of space within the shelf. On the top shelf, the framed print was left in the middle and taller accessories flank both sides of the print. While they are bigger

accessories, they fail to cover much of the vertical height in that shelf's space.

BARB'S COMMENTS: This was a good effort – just not quite good enough, I'm afraid. One thing you don't want to be is too predictable with your arrangements. You also don't want to be overly repetitive. It would have been far more effective to change the number of accessories in each shelf: 1 on one shelf, 3 on another, 5 on another. Why all the same type of accessory? Were there no plants or books or other accessories around? There are too many items in the top shelf, making it appear crowded. If this home was being staged to be sold, there are too many items on the shelf unit period. It looks overly busy and top heavy. The top shelf should also have a white background to eliminate this problem. Overall, some of the accessories should have been taller and I would like to see the quantities varied so as not to so predictable and therefore a bit boring. Very sorry. This could be much better.

Case Study 80

BEFORE
Moving in or moving out? I think the latter. Which would
explain why a professional stager was brought in to help sort
out the mess, determine what needs to be edited out and how
to make this bedroom appear as spacious and relaxing as
possible.

AFTER
Have you noticed the windows were set at different heights?
The stager countered this oddity by running a valance from
left to right over both windows simultaneously. The bed was
then positioned at an angle, using the two windows as a
backdrop. The chest of drawers was moved from in front of
the windows to another place in the room. A simple lace
bedspread and pillow treatment add color in the room. It's
not an elegant room, but then it doesn't have to be. It just

needs to suggest a good arrangement idea for the room and help potential buyers see the benefits of this room for their own purposes.

BARB'S COMMENTS: Honestly there isn't too much to say about this room that I haven't already said. The rumpled throw at the foot of the bed looks too casual and could have been used to make the bed look wider. The framed décor on the wall should be larger; the low chest is much too small.

One of the things about staging and redesign: So long as the arrangements use the homeowners own furnishings, we cannot always command what is used. So we must take what's there and make a room look as useable and as appealing as we can. It's part of the job. It makes it both challenging and gratifying when we are able to succeed, even if there are things we'd rather do differently. Since the windows do not match in size, I probably would not have placed the bed in the corner as it just accentuates this oddity, but still the room does look better than it did before.

Case Study 81

BEFORE
When selling a home, try not to use a table cloth. If the table is in excellent condition, let it shine. Table cloths can get

soiled, wrinkled and their placement disturbed. It is far better to showcase the table whenever possible, especially if it is wood as you'll pick up some extra glow when the light strikes the surface.

AFTER
A professional stager was called in to stage the entire home. In the dining room she immediately saw the need for a large area rug to anchor the beautiful dining set. She removed the table cloth and plant and replaced them with a coordinated table runner and a large bowl of fresh fruit. In the far corner she added some softness with a green plant. Look at how

easy it was to create a more professional, finished and fully decorated room that sizzles, displays some drama and really makes the whole room an entertainer's delight.

BARB'S COMMENTS: I have absolutely no negative comments to make about this room – well, one tiny one. The clock on the wall between the window and the cabinet is not in good proportion to the wall. I would have removed it. See, I said it was minor. Otherwise I think this room is smashing and my highest compliments to the stager who made such an impressive impact with so few changes. Terrific job.
Some might not have wanted to cover that gorgeous wood floor – but I love a beautiful area rug on a wood floor. It is the perfect size for the room and the dining set as well.

Case Study 82

BEFORE
Clearly the homeowners tried to create a workable grouping on the mantel. I'm curious as to why there is no screen on the

fireplace and, as a matter of fact, it appears that the top part of the brick has been scorched – a real cause for alarm. I can imagine this home is situated in very cold climate as it appears the fireplace is used often. But the room needs help.

AFTER
The redesigner has removed all of the photos and other accessories from the mantel. She replaced everything with one single, large framed poster. The grate has been removed and replaced with a stand of multiple red candles. All of the fire wood is gone and so is the barrel. The vertical picture on the wall is down and replaced by a plant. A red area rug was placed on the floor in front of the sofa. The neutral room of

black, gray and white has been pumped up with red accents for a bold statement. The blankets and drinking cup have been removed from the theatre chairs. The room looks clean and nicely arranged and depersonalized by removing the family photos.

BARB'S COMMENTS: I love what the stager did with everything except I would have loved to see the brick cleaned, covered or painted. When trying to sell a house, it does not look good for the fireplace to look as if it burns on the outside as well as the inside. The large poster leaning against the wall is out of scale with the width of the mantel and fireplace. An assortment of tall accessories combined with the art print would have helped immensely. A taller, more robust plant or tree would have balanced better with this visually heavy furniture.

Case Study 83

BEFORE
Unfortunately we don't know what's to the left of this very
large bookcase. Perhaps there's a TV to the left side. Actually
it is a giant entertainment center that wraps completely
around the adjacent wall as well. There is a TV angled in the
left corner (out of sight). So the way the furniture is
configured is not exactly conducive to watching TV. Some
adjustments are to be made which I think you'll appreciate.

AFTER
The sofa has been moved to the far end of the room by the
redesigner or stager. The armless chair and ottoman have
been placed out in the room and closer to the TV. The corner
has been changed out for a tall, decorative grandfather clock
and a taller floor plant. The window treatments have been
removed except for the roll up shades. The shelves have

been totally rearranged and appear to be well designed with a variety of accessories in varying shapes, colors and sizes.

BARB'S COMMENTS: I'm just going to have to trust the stager on this one. I'm uncertain as to whether the chair and ottoman have been placed close enough for a comfortable viewing distance. I know the sofa is much too far away. There seems to be a lot of empty space in the room and I'm not at all certain that this arrangement was the best choice under the circumstances, but then again it might have been the only choice. But I present it here for you to study and see how you feel about it. The accessories above the TV section don't work for me personally.

Case Study 84

BEFORE
This living room has a number of problems but the most
glaring problem is one of too many accessories and poor
placement. A redesigner was hired to rearrange the space
and she was able to do some editing as well. Let's see how
she did and what she did.

AFTER
Two high backed wing chairs from the other side of the room
were switched out with the sofa. A nice equally airy table was
placed between them. The shelf unit in the corner got a
rearrangement as well and the room instantly turned much
more appealing. The throw was removed from the back of
the sofa and the sofa was angled off the opposite wall. There
are still too many accessories and wall décor, making for an
overly busy, cluttered result, however.

BARB'S COMMENTS: The area rug in top photo was not positioned in the middle of the two chairs. So two legs of the left chair sit on the rug, but only one leg of the right chair sits on the rug. Watch out for these kinds of nagging problems. They are so easily avoided if you do. The two pictures flanking the clock (top picture) should have been hung closer to the clock for a tighter grouping.

Case Study 85

BEFORE
An older home with a small living room, this home was going on the market to be sold. The professional stager was invited in to look over the property and add her expertise. Here we have two reproduction prints that have the same color palette, however, they have not been framed alike, so one instantly overpowers the other one, creating an instant imbalance on the wall. The armchair and ottoman look completely out of place, jutting out into the room in such an awkward manner.

AFTER
The stager wisely removed the armchair and ottoman from in front of this wall. Whenever you've got doors nearby, be careful not to force people to walk all the way around furniture in order to move from one side of the room to another. The stager placed a sofa table (console) against the wall and removed the awkwardness and blockage of natural traffic lanes.

BARB'S COMMENTS: While the placement of the sofa table was a great idea, the stager unfortunately left the two framed prints on the wall, right where they were. Now they not only are imbalanced due to color variances, but they now look oppressive as they overpower the table. This is not good. The left print should have been removed and the right print should have been lowered and centered over the table. Remember, I've stated several times these simple rules:

1) Don't let the art's width exceed the furniture below it or it's bound to look top heavy.
2) Hang all artwork close to the furniture over which it is hung so that it appears to be a grouping and not disjointed separate units.
3) Make sure you balance all groupings so that one side does not appear heavier in visual weight when compared with its opposite side.
4) Just because it's there, doesn't mean it has to be kept or used. When staging a home, less is usually more.

Case Study 86

BEFORE
I have a feeling this is not the arrangement that the seller
had while living in the home. Perhaps it was empty and we're

just seeing some props the stager brought in. Or perhaps
these pieces belong to the seller and are just randomly placed
here while packing. Obviously the house must not be put on
the market in this condition.

AFTER
Ultimately the stager placed the room's sofa against the
window and placed the coffee table in front of the sofa. The
dark clock on the wall feels out of place and attracts too
much attention, however. This is unfortunate. It should have
been removed.

BARB'S COMMENTS: Besides the meager look of the room, void of any sort of appeal at all (even after the rearrangement of the furniture), an often overlooked problem is that of the window treatment. Yes, the treatment is clean and let's in plenty of light, but it also looks kind of like a shower curtain pulled across a bath tub. I would have hoped the stager would have replaced it or at least tried to add more sheers to the window so that it looked well gathered and more plush. I actually think there is more fabric in the before picture than the after picture, so I'm wondering if the stager took out the center section, which appears shorter in the before picture than the rest of the fabric.

More fabric would have helped immensely and not added much expense. Perhaps these folks were desperate, I don't know, but when you stage a property, be sure to check out every detail, no matter how minute, especially in your after pictures. These are the pictures that may be used to entice buyers and I fear this picture will only be depressing. They will also end up in a stager's portfolio and may not speak well for the stager's talent. This room is just too austere. In this situation, a little more would have been better.

Case Study 87

BEFORE
Here we have the perennial family photograph wall down a hall. Often the pictures are similar in size and frames but all

too often the placement leaves much to be desired. Designing a wall grouping in the hall is just as important as any other place in the home so great care has to be taken to keep it from looking spotty or overdone. One must also remember there is a big difference between designing a grouping for a hall where there is no furniture below the grouping, and designing a grouping over furniture elsewhere in the home.

AFTER
The redesigner did make a major improvement. For one thing, she did not hesitate to bring in other shapes, sizes and pieces to make a much more interesting grouping. Here we see a framed oval mirror, two shelves, some plants, two multi-picture frames and a lot more depth. This is the type of grouping that would attract one's attention and grab hold and cause one to stop and look and take it all in. So kudos to

the redesigner for that. I'm confident that the homeowner was very pleased with the outcome, though there are a few glitches in the overall design.

BARB'S COMMENTS: I do like this grouping very much. But I have two concerns which I'll share with you. The first concern has to do with the overall height of the mirror. It hangs down too low compared to all the other elements on the wall. This creates a scale issue. A slightly smaller mirror would have been ideal or something else hung below the shelves on either side of the mirror for balance would have helped. The second area of concern is the length of the grouping. It appears to be spread out across the whole wall and makes one feel that the arranger was merely trying to fill the entire wall. There's nothing wrong with breaking this apart and hanging two separate groupings on the same wall. Any time you cover more than 2/3rds the width of the wall you're in danger of having proportional issues develop. You can push it to 3/4th of the wall, but not end to end.

Case Study 88

BEFORE
This near-empty home needed some tender loving care to help it sell quickly and for a higher price. We've got here an

extra long table that presents itself as rather bulky if left completely bare. To draw away the attention from the mass of the table and settle it down in the room, some chairs, accessories, table settings and a tree are just what the doctor ordered.

AFTER
This stager knows what she's doing. Not only did she gather the perfect style of chairs around the table, she was not fearful of choosing bold, tall accessories for the centerpiece. The place settings are also well done. I wish you could see it in color. Beautifully done.

BARB'S COMMENTS: Be a little daring in your designs. One of my complaints about homeowners, sellers and even many stagers and redesigners is that they shy away from larger accessories. Go bold. Be daring. You'll be amazed at how your designs will come alive.

Case Study 89

AFTER
Please note this is an after picture, not a before picture. I'm breaking my pattern here because I really want to drive home the importance of not letting the art overpower the

furniture. This after picture is from the same dining room in Case Study 88. It shows the other wall. Notice how the art is wider than the tray table below. Notice too how there is a significant gap of wall showing between the base of the art and the top of the candle and goblets. I think the choices of accessories are beautiful; I just have a problem with the arrangement for these reasons.

AFTER

In this after picture, you see yet again that the art is spread out until it dramatically exceeds the width of the table beneath it. This is a problem. I recognize there is a sculpture between the two framed images, but can you see how choppy it all looks? Better to have used only one image, centered over the table and moved the sculpture to one side or the other for an asymmetrical grouping and so as not to feel top heavy over the table. This arrangement just isn't as effective as it could have been.

Case Study 90

BEFORE
This beautiful home has a few accessories left behind by the
seller or placed there by the agent or stager. With dramatic

windows and a nice sized fireplace and great hardwood
floors, this room would be any stager's delight to manage. So
let's see how it turned out.

AFTER
The placement of a sofa with large colorful throw pillows
draws you into the room and pulls your attention very
quickly out the back window to a beautiful yard. The
matching end tables and lamps create rhythm in the room
and also add needed unity and harmony to the space. The
seating not only focuses some attention on the great window
and view, but also on the fireplace. An area rug helps define
the seating area. Plants soften the harder features in the

room and tie everything together. The room looks spectacular and completely inviting. Anyone would be proud to own such a home.

BARB'S COMMENTS: Beautifully done! An excellent example to study. This stager has properly directed the buyer's eye to all of the excellent features and benefits of this room. The color palette is current and full of energy. The colors are distributed around the room for balance. I'm not exactly sure why the two ottomans were angled like that at the corner of the rug, but I'm not going to complain. Kudos to the stager! Notice all the clean lines. There's not too much going on, yet it is not sparsely decorated. There's just enough.

Case Study 91

BEFORE
Pictures taken from above are especially unique and helpful
because one can see the depth in the room. This empty
dining room is about to get staged.

AFTER
To anchor the dining room table, the stager brought in a very
large colorful area rug. Set against the dark hardwood floors,
it is rich and well proportioned. Next came the traditionally
styled table and chairs, very suitable for the style of the home
and the neutral color palette. The table has been decorated
with beautiful place settings at every chair. A very large, tall
vase of flowers graces the center of the table. An elegant
decorative beveled mirror is hung centered on the wall which

reflects the beautiful chandelier and the centerpiece. The artwork chosen for the far wall repeats the style of the room, the colors in the room and the ambience of the room.

BARB'S COMMENTS: This is another example of excellence when staging a home. I love everything about it except for the arrangement on the back wall. It looks overdone to my eye. I would prefer a single larger mirror hung in the center without the two outer prints. Or I would have preferred the mirror to be removed, and the framed prints hung close together as companions in the center of the wall. I say once again: Resist <u>filling up</u> the wall with decorative pieces. It just isn't necessary and can easily hurt the overall design of the room. Less on the wall would have been more in this case.

Case Study 92

BEFORE
This layout is interesting because the room's natural focal point, the fireplace, is angled in the room. There are two

patio doors as well, so one must allow easy passage and access to these two areas of the room. The professional stager is on her way – let's see the outcome.

AFTER
A large square area rug is placed in front of the fireplace and at the same angle. This created a beautiful opportunity for the sofa and love seat to work the same angle. The throw pillows are plentiful and help fill up the space or mass of the room with its extra high ceiling. Large, impressive and dramatic framed prints are placed on 3 of the walls: over the fireplace, two on the far right wall (creating a nice vertical alignment similar to the patio doors and the window above),

and on the far left wall over what appears to be a chest or buffet. Color is well distributed around the room for balance. A large tree helps balance the heights in the room from the top of the fireplace picture to the top of the window on the right side of the wall. There is good use of spot lights on the art and tree.

BARB'S COMMENTS: The perfect blend of furniture, art, accessories and plants - and the perfect placement - make this room look outstanding. It is not overdone. It is a joy to see a stager take the challenge and pull a room together with such ease and professionalism. I'm still not that crazy about seeing a sofa half on a rug and half off, but that's me. I think I'll always have a problem with some decisions others find acceptable I suppose.

Case Study 93

BEFORE
This open contemporary home requires considerable
furniture to fill it up to make it inviting enough for buyers.
Two completely separate living areas are adjoined. It's

important that the color palette unite the two separate
spaces and clearly delineate each space. The professional
stager has a huge task to accomplish.

AFTER
Area rugs are one of the best tools a stager or redesigner can
use to define space, provide a more intimate feeling that is
conducive to conversation and help a home look spectacular.
As you can see, there is a separate area rug for the back
section as well as in the foreground. The walls of this great
room are immense. But still the eye needs to be focused on
the living space and not necessarily drawn to the ceiling. In
the foreground setting, two matching arm chairs face the

sofa. A large glass coffee table helps to pull them together. In the back section, a sofa backs to a wall with two matching end tables and matching lamps with a separate coffee table. Dark throw pillows repeat some of the same colors contained in the two abstract paintings hung one above the other on the wall over the sofa.

BARB'S COMMENTS: I have two concerns about the staging of this very large space. In the foreground, we have two dark geometric arm chairs. Opposite them is an off white sofa. I would have liked to see some additional dark pillows on the sofa to balance the area a little better. In the back section, I'm concerned that the two paintings together appear top heavy for the sofa and lead the eye too much toward the ceiling. It's good there are dark pillows on the sofa to add more visual weight at the bottom, but I think the room would have been served better if only the larger of the two paintings were hung on the wall. Other than this (and that too small area rug in the foreground) I think the staging is very, very good.

Case Study 94

BEFORE
This stately home has all the grandeur it could ever hope for.
But as a completely empty space, it would be a huge
challenge for even the most competent home stager.

AFTER
Don't concern yourself with the size, especially with the
height. Bring a buyer's attention down to the actual living
area – that part of the room that is eye level or below. That's
just what the professional stager did here. An area rug
defines the seating arrangement's dimensions. A sofa is
placed facing the fireplace. Two unmatched chairs are
positioned at opposite corners to create that more intimate,
cozy conversational place. All of the components are
connected by the glass coffee table, decorated with a tall,
magnificent floral arrangement. Throw pillows help to
sprinkle color around the space.

BARB'S COMMENTS: A beautiful job. Well done. Still would like to see the chairs fully on the rug, not half on and half off. Matching arm chairs would be preferable for symmetrical balance and better scale in this traditional setting and oversized space.

Case Study 95

BEFORE
This game room lacks cohesiveness and planning. As game rooms go, it is not unusual for them to become messy. I mean, that's sort of expected, right? When staging a home, it is always a good idea to make a space neat and orderly and to even suggest a different usage than one might ordinarily expect.

AFTER
So this game room has received an adult makeover. Not only are the toys gone, but new furniture has been introduced, making this a lovely sitting room or a room suitable for watching TV or doing other family activities.

BARB'S COMMENTS: The stager of this room did an outstanding job. The walls have been painted a pale blue to brighten up the neutral carpet and sofa. The black coffee table provides strong drama and contrast, but needs a larger centerpiece or a large plant. The wall grouping looks casual and well designed, except for the fact it has been hung too close to the end of the wall on the left side. I would have preferred it be more centered on this triangular wall and possibly mimic the angle of the sloping ceiling if possible. I do love the floor lamp and feel overall the room is very well staged.

Case Study 96

BEFORE
Many contemporary homes in affluent communities enjoy
massively spacious rooms. Because they are contemporary
styles, fewer furnishings are required because contemporary,

modern styles embrace minimalism. But still there needs to
be enough in the room to enhance the architecture and help
buyers fall in love with the idea of living in the home.

AFTER
Much of what is needed to stage this room was already in the
room. The furniture needed to be rearranged, obviously. The
configuration chosen is the H-shaped arrangement, where
two matching sofas are placed parallel to each other and
perpendicular to the fireplace. Unnecessary pieces are
removed from the premises. A white area rug defines the size
of the seating arrangement. Unique works of art underscore

the contemporary, modern style. Nothing obstructs the great view of the Pacific Ocean out back. The floors are highly polished and sparkle for that extra gleam.

BARB'S COMMENTS: Another stager who really knows

what's she's doing. This project was masterfully executed. I love every bit of it. The large, strong works of art and sculpture are in keeping with a home of this caliber. The angle of the photograph is exceptional as well. With the figurine looming large in the right foreground, it makes this room look far larger than it actually is, which would really attract potential buyers, especially off the internet.

Case Study 97

BEFORE
An ornate Oriental style area rug or carpet can sometimes
cause complications when it comes to furniture
arrangement. This seller appears to still be living in the home
while boxing things up and preparing for a sale. It was the
home stager's job to make this room come alive and show off
all those built-in shelves.

AFTER
A strong center of interest has been created by the stager
with a white sofa and two matching white (or off white) arm
chairs set side by side across from the sofa. The other colors
in the room (reds, browns, tans) are repeated in the throw
pillows. Plants have been widely and wisely utilized on the
shelves to help break up the space. The stager has not tried

to fill up every single shelf, leaving those at the top either empty or with smaller accessories. Since the visual strength needs to be on the bottom at all times, larger accessories and darker accessories are sprinkled over the lower shelves. A couple of matching wicker boxes double as coffee tables.

BARB'S COMMENTS: This is the type of arrangement which leads the eye straight to the fireplace before allowing it to move to other points in the room. By directing the eye, the stager helps buyer's focus on the natural assets of the room since their furnishings will be quite different from the staged room. Always light the fire before taking the after pictures. The shelving unit might be a little too full for a staged room, but this is another example of a professionally staged room that packs a lot of power.

Case Study 98

BEFORE
Left like this, the bed would feel completely dwarfed in this

room. While the view would always be great, views aren't the only thing that people look at when considering the purchase of a home. The professional stager's job is to add any necessary furniture and accessories that might be needed to make this the most beautiful master bedroom in the area.

AFTER
Notice the massive design and drama created in this space with the beams contrasted with the white ceiling. Now look at how the stager picked up on those geometric lines with the selection of a head board for the bed. This oversized master bedroom has been carefully divided into two sections: the sleeping area and a sitting area. Four matching arm chairs have been placed facing each other on a beautiful white area

rug. A glass table serves as a coffee table. The white throw pillow and rug pull the white from the bed linens over to the opposite side of the room, tying the two sections neatly and beautifully together. This neutral palette is relaxing and will appeal to a great number of buyers. The plants add softness to this beautiful space that is punctuated by the great view of the bay.

BARB'S COMMENTS: This exquisite, luxurious room is an ideal oasis from a busy day's endeavors. I'm captivated by the beautiful way the stager arranged the room and also her choices of furnishings. My only discomfort is that the night stand on the left of the bed sits in front of the window when there is extra wall available on the right side to place the bed in the middle of the wall rather than offset it to the left. Perhaps this placement was just done for the camera, I don't know. I've seen other pictures of the room that indicate there is no reason for the bed to be offset to the left as shown.

Case Study 99

BEFORE
A beautiful double wide brick fireplace is completely hidden in this living room. Packing is well underway as the family

prepares to move out and sell the home. The position of the fireplace makes it imperative to separate this room into two smaller rooms. Let's see what the stager chooses to do.

AFTER
Yep, the room has been divided into two separate sections. A contemporary chair and ottoman have been placed in front of the fireplace, suggesting the perfect spot to read a good book while enjoying a crackling fire on a cold night. An end table (out of sight) supports the reading light. Two companion art prints decorate the fireplace from end to end. An area rug helps to define the space. In the foreground, a beautiful sofa faces the back yard. The supporting pieces are

two matching ottomans and a rectangular coffee table which appears to be in perfect scale with the sofa. Throw pillows pull some of the tan colors up onto the sofa to tie the look together. Beautiful accessories complete the picture making this room a very pleasant room with multiple purposes. The job of a stager is to help potential buyers see all of the advantages and benefits of each and every room in the home. By doing this the stager helps the seller and the agent gain the maximum number of offers on the home that are possible.

BARB'S COMMENTS: I think this room is beautifully arranged. If you could see the colors you would love the soft, neutral palette punched up with a hint of cherry red or rust. I'm a little puzzled by the small tiered table placed just to the right of the arm chair near the fireplace. I think I might have dropped that out of the equation but then it's easy to be picky when you're just looking at photos, which hardly tell the full story. The picture on far right of back wall appears too close to the corner to be framed by the wall adequately.

Case Study 100

BEFORE
Children's rooms are some of the more difficult rooms to

stage, I think. There is usually a ton of stuff everywhere. If the family still lives in the home, it can be really difficult to edit the child's possessions and even harder to get their cooperation to keep the room neat and orderly after the stager is gone. Let's see how this challenge was resolved by the professional stager.

AFTER
The bed placement was not changed. The bed was made and the protective sides were removed to give the appearance of being occupied by an older child. The corner chest of drawers was moved to the opposite wall, and the extra toys or furniture on the far left of the room were no doubt packed up and removed entirely. All that remains is the shelf unit under

the window. Dark faux draperies were hung to make the room appear larger, with higher ceiling but instead tend to overpower the room. An area rug helps to define the area. A chest with a cushion doubles as a bench. Notice how the poster of the horse faces into the room and not out of the room. This directional piece helps to draw the attention of the buyers toward the bed. The colors in the pillows and the dark trim on the area rug help to distribute the dark colors around the room for balance.

BARB'S COMMENTS: This room developed into a very charming, attractive space. There is just enough left to make it appear as if the child still lives in the room, but there is no clutter, no messiness, and no junk lying around anywhere. I would have wished the rods for the panel drapes were shorter and not so noticeable and the drapes a lighter color. Other than that, I think the stager did an outstanding design for this room.

Case Study 101

BEFORE
One's perspective can sure change depending on the angle of
a photograph. Always remember this. It's one of the reasons,
as a professional stager and redesigner I make sure I take a
sizeable number of pictures before I go to work and then
once again after I'm finished. Case in point: Look at the

white recessed area left of the fireplace in the before shot
(taken from the right side of the room). Now compare that to
the size of that same area as shown from the left side of the
room in the after picture (next page). Does it not look much
wider in the after picture, particularly because the artwork is
wide but not very tall? The room in the after picture also
looks much, much larger than it does in the before picture,
and the after picture is filled with furniture while the before
picture is virtually empty. One's vantage point is super
important when taking pictures. Pictures can make or break

a sale because nowadays so many buyers search online long
before they actually show up at a home to view it personally.

AFTER
Always take pictures from all four corners of a room, both
before you start work and after you are done. Look for the
best angles to display the focal point and the furniture's
relationship to the focal point or any other asset the room
gives, like this absolutely fabulous view overlooking the
coastline. Choose colors that enhance the home, that are in
keeping with the style of the home as well as the furniture
and accessories. Strive to stay up-to-date with changing
interior colors and combinations. Look for ways to romance
a room with artful accessories. Stock up on large accessories
for the greatest impact in your staging pictures. Look for
unusual ways of arranging the furniture for that WOW effect.
Try not to be predictable. Challenge your creativity. And
most of all: Have fun and enjoy your work.

CHAPTER 3

LEARNING FROM THE SUCCESS AND FAILURE OF OTHERS

So there you have it – 101 Case Studies – examples of actual rooms that have been staged or re-arranged by a professional home stager or interior redesigner. I've shown you results that were disappointing when compared to what they could have been. I've shown you results that were very good but could have been improved upon with minor adjustments. And I've shown you results that were stunning needing little to no adjustment whatsoever.

In each Case Study, I've looked for new or repeated problems. I know that in some cases the critiques eventually got a bit redundant, but that's because there are some arrangement mistakes commonly made by a large group of people, even after they have been trained. So therefore it seems warranted to hammer home some of these issues. They are important. Cautiously avoiding them will only help your personal results as you stage or redesign your own home or the homes of your clients. In any educational process, repetition is a necessary component to successful retention and application.

Arranging furniture and accessories at a professional level is both easy and difficult. There are many factors that play a role in determining the best course of action. There are many options – or there might be very few options. Professional stagers and redesigners need to learn to be flexible and adaptable and yet, all the while, they must keep the end goals of the client in mind. After all, it does no one any good if the client is unhappy or their goals are not achieved. And a stager's or redesigner's reputation is on the line. By making sure you are functioning at the top level in the industry, you will go a long way to establishing your self as a true professional and worthy of your hire.

Anyone can start a business. Anyone can offer a solution. But not everyone can sustain a business for the long term. Without strong design or arrangement skills, it will be very difficult (if not impossible) to sustain a business in this very visual industry. Success breeds success. You can have all the best organizational skills, marketing methods and promotional aids in the industry. But the proof is in the pudding, as they say. You will ultimately be judged on the final outcome of the rooms you work on. You will be judged on the visual impact and the functionality of each room. So by applying what you have learned and always seeking to improve your knowledge and skills, you will give yourself every conceivable advantage over those who don't.

As competition for these services strengthens around the country and around the world, your personal reputation may make or break your business. I've written extensively on the business side of starting and building a strong business, and this book helps to fill in some of the missing gaps on the design side of things.

It is my hope that you have found this excursion to be helpful in clarifying concepts you may have been confused by, or in teaching you concepts you never learned before. And whether you totally agree with my assessments or not, I hope I've caused you to think more deeply, think more wisely, and think more aesthetically. One of the great things about creativity is that it allows one to explore new ideas, new techniques, and new concepts. It allows one to consider breaking traditional rules and ideas. But if you're going to break some of the *rules*, you've first got to know what the rules are in order to break them successfully. You don't want to just break rules out of lack of knowledge or with wild guesses. As time permits, I may write a sequel to this book with even more Case Studies from my files. But for now I think this book, when coupled with my ebook on arrangement techniques (Décor Secrets Revealed), and together with my workbook (Arrange Your Stuff) and my wall groupings book (Wall Groupings! How to Arrange Your Photos and Art), provide any reader with virtually all of the helpful guidance to master the art of arranging furniture and accessories.

I want to thank you for taking this trip with me. My thanks to all my wonderful certified students for the examples provided via their portfolios and the lessons learned from their hard work. They are the real success stories because they have let nothing stop them from achieving success, even if they have struggled in the beginning or along the way. In every case, they have proven that anyone can learn – that anyone, regardless of age or background or experience can develop their skills and achieve a high level of competence in an area of design that few have bothered to learn. They are to be commended and applauded.

One is never too old to learn. One is never too old to improve. One is never too old to try something new.

If you're not reading this book because you have or want to have a business of your own, and you're now excited about getting in the industry with your own business, please read through the additional resources in the next chapter, which provide details to courses, other books, visual aids and tools that will help you achieve all your goals, whatever they may be.

Best wishes and success in your decorating.

Barbara Jennings, CSS/CRS - Founder and Director
The Academy of Staging and Redesign
Decorate-Redecorate.Com

CHAPTER 4

WHERE TO FIND ADDITIONAL TRAINING, VISUAL AIDS, TOOLS AND RESOURCES

Courses You Can Take

Many real estate agents decide at some point that they are more interested in serving clients as professional stagers rather than continuing as agents. After reading this book, you may feel that way as well. Since the material I cover in this book is only a portion of what professional stagers typically learn, anyone considering a career change is advised to take additional training in the design and business structures needed for success as professional stagers running a business.

Training opportunities now abound – some good and some not so good. In all matters, take time to investigate before choosing.

There are, of course, others who offer seminars and workshops. They usually require your attendance for 5 days. Prices are dramatically higher for this type of "hands-on" training and, depending on your location, you might have to travel a considerable distance to attend and pay for lodging while there. Typically when taking a seminar, you'll be required to sign an agreement to abide by the association's rules (which may easily infringe on your independence) and there are usually hefty annual renewal fees you'll have to pay.

The quality of the seminar and the training is dependent on who conducts the seminar, not its founder. Many do not include <u>design</u> or <u>arrangement</u> training as part of their seminar, claiming staging is not decorating and that it is part of the real estate industry not the design industry. But facts are facts and failure to teach design dramatically weakens a stager's effectiveness out in the field.

There are also online, <u>web-based</u> courses or <u>combination-style</u> courses (such as my own – consisting of ebooks, books, visual aids, tools and online training). Some require you to take all of the training online with strict deadlines and there are always hefty annual fees to pay to retain access to the training and anything associated with it (like a website). Some offer design training and some do not. For myself, I decided early on to be **student centered** first and foremost, so I do <u>not</u> charge renewal fees for training. The only forward going fees I charge are for website renewals because I am charged renewal fees by the third party entities that host the websites. These fees are minimal, however.

Again it is important to investigate your options thoroughly before choosing the training style that is right for you. It is also important to investigate the reputation of the trainers to see how long they have been in business, their company's Better Business Bureau rating, their testimonials, their designations, whether they provide design training or not, their visual aids, tools and so forth (if any). You want to make sure the company you train with has an excellent reputation and, if seeking a designation, offers a designation that enjoys the highest respect. Notice I did not say the designation that is the most well known. Being well known should not be the major criteria for determining quality, integrity and respect.

For those interested in my highest value course as of this writing, please visit this webpage for complete details:

http://www.decorate-redecorate.com/diamond-ruby-combo-course.html

This course includes comprehensive training in the home staging AND interior redesign industries for anyone wishing to start their own business. It will solidify your confidence in both design and business structure, provide you with essential visual aids that will help you promote your business from day one, and provide you with extremely handy tools that make furniture movement super easy. The course **includes** a student's certification fee, a lifetime access to the Diamond private training website, two lifetime directory listings, a brochure website, newsletters, personal advice, a discussion forum, your own personal reference library, some valuable ebooks and much, much more. Please note, this course is subject to change without notice. For the most up-to-date information on anything I offer, please visit my website. Payment plans are also available.

Books You Can Acquire

For many, taking advantage of a course offers the highest degree of comprehensive training and support and the most value for their investment. They would be right. However, not everyone has the resources or time to take this route. Happily there are other options. Following are a listing of ebooks and books that I have written which are also available "a la carte" for your convenience. Full details are available on each one at my website so I'll only provide a brief snippet here.

Business Training by the Author

Home Staging for Profit gives readers a clear and precise guide to opening, growing and maintaining a successful home staging <u>business</u>. There is a huge amount of additional, in-depth training, as well as extremely handy business forms, business start-up guidance and so much more. It is 256 pages of incredibly detailed how-to information in a large sized format (8.5x11) and is currently my best selling manual (also available in ebook format). For specific details please visit my website.

Home Staging in Tough Times is a sequel to the book above. It was developed at the onset of our economic recession and is packed full of guidance on how to survive and grow a staging business during down markets. It has many actual examples of marketing tactics and strategies readers can use, a plethora of forms to make the process easier and approaches staging from a completely different mindset one would normally use. It too is a large format manual (8.5x11) and consists of 209 pages. No one else offers this type of training unless they gleaned it from this one-of-a-kind book written just for this market in the industry.

Staging Luxurious Homes is for professional stagers who want to specialize in upper class homes and working with agents who serve affluent neighborhoods. It is packed with details about the different ways wealthy people think and act, how to network with them, how to serve them, and how to grow a staging business as a confident professional within this specialized group. This 217 page guide is unique in the industry and comes in a 6x9 format.

Getting Paid for Home Staging focuses on how to protect a staging business from unscrupulous consumers who try to avoid paying for services after they have been rendered. It is a layman's look at steps the reader can take to minimize trouble before it starts. It covers staging ethics, tricks of the trade to enhance a home and much more. It is offered in a 6x9 format and is 191 pages.

Staging Portfolio Secrets offers step by step procedures in creating a powerful, unique and in-depth staging and redesign portfolio that will help readers gain new clients. It is highly applicable to agents as well. It helps stagers decipher their most engaging and useful talents from their past and present, and add them to the mix of photos, certificates, statistics and other valuable data that should be part of every portfolio – the kind of information that easily sets the reader ahead of the competition. This 263 page manual in 6x9 format includes many forms, photo examples and more.

Rearrange It teaches you how to break into the interior redesign industry. Closely related to home staging, redesign helps consumers enjoy their homes more fully by professionally arranging furniture and accessories they already own. This manual is an excellent business guide covering all the essential information about setting up a business, marketing the services, doing consultations and full redesign services. While many of the concepts are similar to or the same as for home staging, there are specific differences because the end results are drastically different for the clients. It is offered in 8.5x11 format of 176 pages or as an electronic book.

Advanced Redesign provides top of the line additional products and services a professional stager or redesigner could offer to their clients to expand and leverage their profits to the max. It is considered advanced training and definitely a consideration to employ after you get your business up and running. With 212 pages devoted to this subject, you're sure to find great ideas to enhance your business and benefit clients. The book comes in 8.5x11 format.

A Real Estate Agent's Guide to Offering Free Home Staging Advice (or Consultations) While not meant at all to replace the value and work of professional home stagers, this guide is written to realtors to acquaint them with the

concept and value of hiring professional stagers. It clarifies staging concepts and services, offers them direction in how to find local stagers and gives them practical tips they can offer to sellers when staging services are out of the question. It is not meant for the general public nor for those seeking to offer staging as a business. The book is 6x9 and 234 pages.

The Best Consultation Aid You'll Find

Home Staging for Yourself is an incredibly handy consultation aid for both you and your seller. It is the most thorough checklist ever developed to assist an agent, a stager or a seller inspect and compile a list of tasks that need to be addressed for every conceivable part of a home, both inside and outside. Written to the seller, each area or room of a typical home is separated out and the most common tasks that stagers address are identified for each area or room. Blank lines are also included for each room or area so that each booklet can be customized to the particular situation, making it the first and only booklet of its kind that makes organizing the vital tasks easy to follow and understand – while making the process completely customizable on the spot, saving everyone who uses it valuable time and effort.

The current edition is 105 pages in a 5x8 format. Stagers and agents can purchase these useful to-do lists, professionally printed in small quantities at discounted prices and pass them on to the seller for free or a modest up-charge. When up-charging for the checklist guides the guides become a small profit center for the agent or stager or a value added product offered to a seller to gain a listing. Complete details on the value and usefulness of these checklists are at http://www.decorate-redecorate.com/home-staging-for-yourself.html

Furniture Moving and Lifting Tools

No matter what your age or physical conditioning, it's important to use safety measures when moving heavy furniture to protect your spine and muscles. Should you decide to involve yourself in assisting sellers in rearranging furniture, you'll definitely appreciate our **Furniture Moving and Lifting Set**.

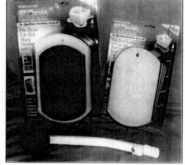

Stagers routinely use these types of tools. A set would make a <u>great client gift</u> to the seller, but they'll need it prior to staging the home. I advise all stagers to have several sets of carpet and floor sliders plus the all-steel, portable lifter. The set and extra sliders are available from my website at http://www.decorate-redecorate.com/furniture-lifter.html

Design Training by the Author

<u>Décor Secrets Revealed</u> is 25 chapters on the full scope of properly arranging furniture and accessories just like the pros. As I stated earlier, the design training in this manual covers some of the most essential concepts you should know. However, it should be noted that it is <u>not</u> sufficient for anyone wishing to offer professional staging or redesign services. To fully learn all the tactics, rules and practices that interior designers use when arranging furniture, accessories and art, this electronic book is vital to your core training. It is chocked full of full color photographs (over 600) and comes in a downloadable ebook. You will learn virtually everything you need to know (and then some) and it will provide readers with the confidence to give solutions equal to any expert and give authoritative answers when clients ask questions regarding furniture and accessory arrangement.

Arrange Your Stuff

This workbook is the sequel to my ebook above. It is a compilation of many rooms that have been professional arranged – and in many cases you'll see 2 or more examples of how the room could have been arranged using the same furniture and accessories that the client already owned. By studying other options

for a room, stagers and redesigners learn to think outside the box, learn to be flexible with their arrangement choices, and learn how to offer alternatives to their clients down the road when the client has tired of the arrangement they initially received. Many people carry this workbook in their vehicle, so when at a client's home they can quietly slip out to their car for a refresher should they encounter a difficult room. In this manual I give you a line drawing of the room as the client had arranged the furniture prior to the appointment, then I give you a drawing of the rearranged room after the service was rendered, and when possible, up to 2-4 additional drawings of how the room could have also been

arranged, all equally nice. This comb-bound workbook is 8.5x11 and 189 pages.

Wall Groupings! Secrets of Displaying Your Art and Photos

is the sequel to a book I published in the 1980's. This 147 page book in 5x8 format is loaded with photos of all sorts of wall groupings from simple to complex. It includes all of the concepts readers should know when it comes to creating a beautifully arranged grouping, plus instructions on how to properly hang the groupings. It should be noted that this training is not especially essential for stagers and agents as staged homes generally do not include elaborate wall groupings, however it never hurts to learn this specialized training not available anywhere else.

Where to Get Our Current Training and Even More Resource Aids and Tools

For a complete list of current ebooks, books and up-to-the-minute courses (including full training in the home staging or interior redesign or corporate art consulting fields), plus all of the exclusive visual aids, tools of the trade and a huge selection of free decorating tips, please visit my flagship website:

http://www.decorate-redecorate.com

Our product catalog is located at:

http://www.decorate-redecorate.com/catalog.html

For Information About Certification

Please check our website for current information about certification <u>for agents</u> as well as professional stagers and redesigners. We offer the following highly respected professional designations:

CSS (Certified Staging Specialist)
CRS (Certified Redesign Specialist)
CREHSA (Certified Real Estate Home Staging Advisor)

JUST A FEW TESTIMONIALS

"I have prayed for months for God to lead me to the right Staging Certification training, and I can't express how very blessed I feel stumbling upon this program. First off, I am so impressed with the way Ms. Jennings and her staff replied to my emails whenever I had a question about training. It was always the same day that they returned my emails. Not many companies do that. Also, I know a friend of mine that took another certification course a couple years ago (3 day seminar), she paid $1700 and told me that she did not learn hardly anything on the design aspect of home staging! I was dumbfounded. . . . Being accountable, in my opinion, is why this program stands out above the competition. . . . - **Nancy King, Clayton, NC**"

"I just finished reading Home Staging for Profit and was extremely pleased with the details and comprehensive nature of the book. - **Diane Dove**"

" . . . Barbara Jennings is a very talented individual and is proud to put her name behind the stagers she trains, because she knows first hand if you have the ability. I highly recommend her........she is a wealth of knowledge and is so willing to share it. I think you will be very pleased to take your career in her direction. Good luck! - **Barb Combs & Chanda Humphries, Added Touches Inc.**"

"I went on the Net searching for someone in my area. Quite honestly, I can't imagine how you can get a Certificate within a weekend/week and what was being touted on the various websites. I found that confusing and hard to believe that after a weekend you could walk away and be able to handle any situation that came your way. I was looking for some one to really teach me the trade so that I could actually be of real use to my clients. . . . I next went to Amazon.com to order a couple of books and Barbara's name popped up and I ordered two of her books to get the feeling for the industry. I really enjoy the way Barbara writes. Yes, give it to me in black and white; tell me it again and in different ways how and why certain layouts and percentages are called for. I come from a financial background where it is all about getting your License/Certification. The online help and Barbara's attitude said to me ....this is where I will get good fundamentals to start with and a great back-up team if I need an answer to a question. It is very rare today that an owner is willingly available to students. Last but not least I did look her up on BBB and thought, now this is some one that I would be proud to learn from. - **Esther Rhein**"

CPSIA information can be obtained at www.ICGtesting.com
Printed in the USA
LVOW05s1841301113

363342LV00002B/435/P